MW00483454

"HAVING AN *Affair?*"

A HANDBOOK FOR THE *"Other Woman"*

SARAH J. SYMONDS

Red Brick Press
New York

Red Brick Press
An Imprint of Hatherleigh Press
5-22 46th Avenue, Suite 200
Long Island City, NY 11101
www.hatherleighpress.com

Library of Congress Cataloging-in-Publication data available upon request.
ISBN 978-1-57826-279-3

All Red Brick Press titles are available for bulk purchase, special promotions, and premiums. For information about reselling and special purchase opportunities, please call 1-800-528-2550 and ask for the Special Sales Manager.

Cover and interior design and layout by Lee Lewis Walsh, Words Plus Design, www.wordsplusdesign.com

The author can be contacted through her website, www.havinganaffairthebook.com

10 9 8 7 6 5 4 3 2 1
Printed in the United States of America

Few love to hear the sins they love to act.

William Shakespeare,
Pericles, Act 1, Scene 1

Dedication

**To all those who contributed toward
my research for this book**

*(you all know who you are,
even if you don't want anybody else to!)*

Contents

Acknowledgments

Thank you to my wonderful family and friends for your constant love and support, as well as your belief in me and in my ability to make *"Having An Affair?"* happen. An extra special thank you to my big brother Mark, for his constant life coaching, honest critique and unique "scheming services." Never judgmental and always there for me — you are a great man *and* a great friend.

I would like to thank Lee Lewis Walsh of Words Plus Design for her dynamic vision (and *extreme* patience) in helping me present this book to the world. You have never uttered the word "no" to me, and for that I am extremely grateful.

To my darling hairdresser Scott Thompson, the man with the sharpest scissors in Hollywood! You were right — blondes really *do* have more fun. Thank you for my "look," as well as our laughter and quasi-psychotherapy salon sessions. We will always be friends — *you know too much!*

A special thank you to my dear friends Lola and Sizzler for the incessant phone debates about our cheating married bastards, along with the laughter, tears and juicy information that goes with the territory. What a support group!

Also, on behalf of "other women" around the world, I would like to thank liquor manufacturers and retailers everywhere. You are a staple requirement in a mistress's turbulent life!

(P.S.: Mum, thank you for your secret critique and editing services when Dad wasn't looking — D.T.Y.F!)

Preface

 "Having An Affair?" is not a guide on *how* to have an affair, but more a manual of everything a woman involved with a married man should know. It is essentially *The Other Woman's Handbook.*

Written candidly, with humor and brutal honesty, this no-nonsense self-help book offers insight on the scenario of being one half of an affair. The advice and the handy *"sin-tillating"* tips provided aim to keep the mistress in charge of the relationship and of the situation in general (as well as her sanity), in an effort to minimize the possibility of *her* being the one who gets hurt, as somebody inevitably will—and it isn't typically the lying, cheating, adulterous bastard of a husband!

I can't bear to hear another story—or personally endure the temporary martyrdom again myself—without writing this tome. I owe it to all of you who shared your hundreds of combined years of adulterous dating experiences with me, and as a testament to fellow mistresses dying to see the material in print. Enough already! Let's wake up!

So read, enjoy, and above all *benefit* from "other women's" true stories of confusion, frustration, despair, and misery—stories they were gracious enough to share with me openly and honestly.

USEFUL NOTES TO REMEMBER:

TO MISTRESSES: Life is a negotiation; an affair is an even greater one.

TO WIVES: Marriage is a war.

TO MEN: For many men, marriage is a war against their longings.

The "Induction"

Mistresses' Survival Course is Now in Session

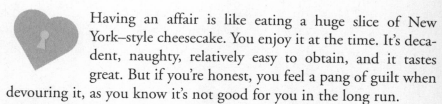 Having an affair is like eating a huge slice of New York–style cheesecake. You enjoy it at the time. It's decadent, naughty, relatively easy to obtain, and it tastes great. But if you're honest, you feel a pang of guilt when devouring it, as you know it's not good for you in the long run.

For those of you dating a married man, who believe you can one day have an honest relationship with him, be aware. Be very aware. Trying to establish trust and honesty in a relationship born of an affair with a cheater is as likely to succeed as choosing a babysitter from a pedophilia support group!

Single women who get entangled with married men are the ones who really suffer. They are the ones left with a broken heart and an empty void when the affair ends, while the husband usually goes back to a forgiving wife and children. (Typical scenario: a family holiday to Disney World and a few opportune Hail Marys, then *bingo!* He's back in the fold.)

The essence of this book is to highlight the importance of a mistress being prepared and on top of things (in more ways than one) at all times—to eliminate her making excuses for his duplicitous actions and to empower her to start taking some action of her own.

"HAVING AN *Affair?*"

This is a revolutionary book, and the research associated with it covers most, if not all, of the main topics relating to extramarital affairs—from enjoying some of the most hedonistic liaisons (with somebody else's husband) to surviving the fallout from the nastiest affair, and from how to engineer being spoiled like a princess to knowing when to drop-kick that deadweight, cheapskate married lover.

A tongue-in-cheek, cynically instructive handbook highlighting situations that all women who choose to embark on an affair will experience at some time, it is a crucial guide to everything a potential or current mistress should know about affairs, men and their marriages, and (most crucially) men and their lies.

Throughout the book I will be sharing information and offering sizzling advice by way of my "notes" and "tips" to you all, and addressing particular categories of readers as required.

As a result of my extensive research, I no longer associate marriage with monogamy. I now associate it with the alienation of affection, which is often followed by divorce. Of course this is not true of all marriages. *(Just most.)*

I will be taking a direct and realistic, non-venomous look at the whole society-sensitive subject of having an affair. I say society-sensitive because affairs always have to be kept secret, don't they? I mean, c'mon—if a single woman who is having an affair is at a social gathering, and during general cocktail conversation is asked the question of her status (i.e., whether she is single, dating, or engaged), she is hardly going to pipe up proudly and say, "Oh yes. Yes, I am dating. I'm having a wonderful affair with Mrs. Smith's husband." Or even, "Well, yes, actually I am seeing someone, but he's married so I can't really say too much about it." The result would be gaping mouths and instant judgmental whispering and sneering, but even more demoralizing to the mistress would be the humiliation of hearing her own words said out loud, reminding her of just what a failure she already feels like for settling for so little.

✎ **NOTE TO MISTRESSES:** You are not a failure, but you are settling for much less than you deserve. And you know it, even if you do pretend to be in denial.

⚷ **HANDY SOCIAL CHITCHAT TIP:** For those awkward social occasions, just say you're single and that you're still looking for the right man (that's not a lie, is it?). But do be ready to fend off dumbfounded responses (especially if you're hot) of "How on earth can you be single?" "But you're so fabulous!" And of course the inevitable "What's wrong with men these days!" Be aware that this will quickly be followed by well-intentioned but insistent offers to hook you up with their single male colleagues from the I.T. department.

✎ **NOTE TO SELF:** Why *are* men in I.T. always so single and available?

At the end of the day, why is talking about having an affair so socially taboo and dangerously off limits? Are we scared that someone might actually know Mrs. Smith and tell her? (So many Mrs. Smiths, so little time!) Or are we scared of looking like a loser—and a "loose woman"—in the eyes of the cocktail party "chattee" with whom we are engaging?

It's a smidge hypocritical, don't you think? After all, *everybody* seems to be having affairs these days. And if they're not, then they certainly know of somebody who is. So just why is so much of it going on? Why are there so many unhappily married, incompatible, duplicitous people in the world? People who said "I do" at the altar but really meant "I don't and I never will!" This book will answer all these questions and more.

I recently discovered there are websites available that offer a secret, illicit dating service that enables married men and women to cheat on their partners more easily. Charming!

The whole notion of having an affair tends to be associated with clandestine liaisons and urgent passion, although it often fails to address the other side of the scenario, namely the falsehoods that are created and the pain that inevitably results.

An affair is synonymous with excitement—the adrenaline rush that comes with the risk of doing something wrong—because, let's face it, married men who stray typically do so because they're looking for something more exciting than being with a woman whose biggest goal is to have breakfast in bed together at the weekend, complete with boisterous kids jumping all over them for good measure.

More importantly, however, this book examines why women (a.k.a. mistresses) choose to be involved with an unavailable man in the first place. Why do they make that ultimately destructive decision? How could any sane woman (especially if she is single and the dating world is her oyster) possibly want to resort to being second best in a relationship? Does she have *so* little self-esteem?

✎ **NOTE TO INSANE MISTRESSES:** Are we involved with married men due to the fact there are so very few honest, successful, rich, straight single men available out there? (Just take a look at the nauseating selection on Match.com, for example, if you are in any doubt whatsoever.) Does this supply shortage mean we have to snag other women's husbands just to survive? Or are women who choose to date married men living in denial of severe commitment phobia and therefore are only attracted to complications?

"Having An Affair?" will take a balanced look at just why a man strays from his wife and his marital bed to begin with. Why he has the vigor and virility to cheat but not the same tenacity to actually leave his "other half." I have substantiated my argument with reliable feedback from unhappy, frustrated, adulterous bed-hopping husbands.

The forthcoming pages are filled with real-life experiences, stories, and anecdotes from articulate, attractive, successful women (and a few men, too). All of which are too good not to be "aired and shared" and are too unbelievable to have been made up. It's a sassy, palatable, "facts laid bare" look at the whole business of having an affair from the beginning of the tryst right through to the breakup.

If you're a woman who has been there, currently are there, or might be planning to go there (and yes, even if you have bought the

T-shirt), you'll wish you'd read this book years ago and eliminated the time you wasted on being with the wrong man.

✎ **OBSERVATIONAL NOTE OF LOW PROBABILITY:** Conversely, your affair may be the best thing that ever happened to you and you wouldn't change things for the world.

✎ **NOTE TO SELF:** Yeah, right! This scenario is extremely unlikely, but I have to acknowledge the fact, as I wouldn't want to come across as bitter and twisted now, would I?!

I've discovered in life, mainly through trial and heaps of error, that it pays to be cynical. If you're cynical, you are rarely ever disappointed. So, mistresses, whether you choose to rev it up or put the brakes on your affair, after reading this book you should at least feel well prepared for what it might throw at you, and be savvy enough to cut through the bullshit catalog of lies a married man is feeding you. (And he does have one for each season, by the way.)

To eliminate any doubt, my advice to you—for the record—is not to enter into an affair to begin with and to get out of any affair you may currently be having. You can't really be in love with or respect a man who is cheating on his wife, can you? Doesn't that make him somewhat of a coward and a fraud?

✎ **NOTE TO MISTRESSES:** Even if you ever did end up with him, how could you trust that he wouldn't do the same to you in the future? After all, if he did it *with you,* he could certainly do it *to you!*

But alas, if it's too late, and you are already emotionally knee-deep into an affair with a married man, this book will help you. And the first thing you need to do is be real enough to know that he is the one having it all, not you!

Admit to yourself that you're the one who is bound to suffer and that you are putting yourself in a vulnerable position. With that in mind at the outset, and if it's still your intent to go ahead, I would advise you—off the record—to make sure you're getting something of quality out of your affair. Something that will enrich and bring joy to your life, not just suck it dry emotionally, physically, and mentally.

Even if it's "only" great sex, a promotion at work, or a bit of help with the deposit on that new car, get something for yourself, *please.* Just to offset that gnawing feeling of being "second best" that will unfortunately come as "second nature" to you as the affair progresses.

Without realizing it, you'll become accustomed to the low self-esteem you experience whilst you quite literally accept being second best. The more affairs you have, the more it may lead you to feel that you're just not worthy of an honest relationship with an available man at all.

✎ MENTAL HEALTH WARNING NOTE TO MISTRESSES: In an affair where you are in love, and you care for your married man very much, some level of pain will become part of your daily norm.

If you are one of the many mistresses hoping that your married man will leave his wife for you, good luck.

Although, think on this—if he does end up "marrying the mistress," he is in fact creating an immediate vacancy for a new one.

✎ NOTE OF LIGHT HUMOR TO READERS: What's the definition of a wife who knows where her husband is every night?

ANSWER: A widow!

"HAVING AN *Affair?*"

chapter 1

Unfaithful!

The Adulterer in Action

 The definition of "affair" in the *Collins English Dictionary* is: "sexual relationship outside of marriage." For those of you who have chosen to buy, borrow, or sneak a look at this book, thank you. I truly hope it will be of value to you. It may shock, appall, or intrigue you. At the very least I hope it makes you laugh (even cringe or squirm) and that you may learn something in the process.

✎ **NOTE TO READERS:** If this book inspires you to identify a substandard entanglement you are presently, unhappily, existing in, and it further fills you with the courage to make changes, then my work here is done.

I imagine you to be a woman having an affair with a married man, considering having one, or having had one at some point in your life. I wouldn't be surprised if you bought this book at the airport, perhaps on your way to or from an assignation with your married lover.

You might even be the married man yourself, sneaking a peek at this book while your mistress isn't looking. If that's the case, then boy will you learn a lot!

✎ **NOTE TO UNSEEING MISTRESSES:** I urge you not to let that happen. Hide the book. Don't ever let him learn your tricks and be one step ahead of you.

So, ladies, you could be in the midst of a wonderful, all-consuming extramarital affair and having the time of your life. Or you may be recovering from the hurt and humiliation caused by your involvement with a married man, especially one you've loved and hung on for in despair, believing he would leave his wife for you. Well, why on earth wouldn't he? If he loved you as much as he said he did, how could he possibly bear to be away from you or risk losing you? *(It just doesn't seem to make any logical sense, right?)*

✓ **REALITY CHECK FOR MISTRESSES:** C'mon, sisters, it makes a lot of sense. Are you kidding me? If he really felt as strongly about you as he professes (especially when he wants sex), he would move heaven and earth, and heaven again, to be with you and only you. And let's face it, if he isn't making the moves to leave his wife while you two are hot and heavy for each other, then he is never going to do it, period! Sorry, I know you don't like to hear it, but it's true, and it's better to deal with the truth now than the pain later.

Notwithstanding my seemingly harsh approach in certain areas of this book, you will find support if you've been hurt, advice if you're a novice, and just plain similarities and experiences that you will *so* be able to relate to.

✎ **NOTE TO MISTRESSES:** If you are in the middle of an emotionally draining affair, if you are being used and your spirit is being crushed, this book will be your intervention—your wake-up call! You will find it intoxicatingly liberating, trust me. (And by the way, if your spirit is being crushed, isn't that enough of a wake-up call to know you have to move on and find someone who doesn't want to make a frappé out of your soul?)

Should you happen to be the wife of a man whom you suspect is having an affair, my advice to you is to stop reading now. Your time would be far better spent making your husband happy so that he doesn't feel the need to stray. That is unless, like a large percentage of married women, you've become indifferent.

Unfaithful!
The Adulterer in Action

✎ **NOTE TO WIVES:** Did you know that the opposite of love isn't hate? It is actually indifference.

Let me make it crystal clear before we go any further that I am not advocating affairs. I truly believe that one of the most beautifully satisfying and fulfilling things in life is to be one half of a happy, loving, supportive, honest marriage, or a committed, exclusive relationship. A situation where two people choose to be together, not convince themselves they *have* to stay together due to feeble excuses like kids, finances, property, blah blah blabbity blah. (I'm yawning here just writing it.)

By the way, and you may think this a smidge hypocritical, but for the record, I have zero tolerance for cheating in a "normal" relationship. There is not one line or excuse that could ever fly with me in order to forgive an adulterer and take him back into my arms, *let alone my bed.* If he cheats, it means he's unhappy, and if he's unhappy, let him go. In fact, help him pack his damned bags and be done with it!

✎ **NOTE TO READERS STILL WITH ME SO FAR:** I don't mean to sound hypocritical or sanctimonious here, because when all is said and done I do know we all get into situations and relationships that feel right (or wrong) at the time. Even when we know it's doomed, destructive, or will hurt other people, we don't care; we still do it (sometimes we do it even more). I am the last person to judge! I am merely telling you my ideals and standards for an exclusive relationship, that's all.

As I've said, my aim here is not to teach you how to have an affair, nor am I recommending that you should have one. My goal is purely to reach out to single women who have chosen to be involved with a married man (or even worse, those who have been misled by him and fallen into that scenario), all those women who could be feeling a bit lost, not knowing what to believe any more, as well as those who have already moved into the next phase, and are raging with anger and frustration.

✎ **NOTE OF DEMOGRAPHIC INTENTION:** I refer predominantly to single women, because if you're a married woman having an affair with a married man, you have a whole other load of issues, which I have no interest in exploring here. (Although if you happen to be a married woman having an affair with a single man, I must commend you. Well done and good luck—if you can't beat your husband, then join him, I say!)

This book is intended for women who need some guidance and support but have a hard time discussing the subject with anyone. Friends, especially married ones, find it extremely hard to provide non-judgmental advice on this subject. You soon learn who your real friends are when you decide to have an affair—even more so when it comes to an end. (And boy do they ever love to say, "I told you so!")

I hope my insights and opinions on men, how they think, and how they view relationships, will resonate with *all* women. My purpose is to help you see things more clearly, whatever your status in the relationship game.

✎ **NOTE OF IRONY:** Who knows, it might even help the odd man, too. Although he would *never* admit it, I'm sure.

If you are a woman currently "enjoying" an affair and you have your emotions in check, I wish you luck and happiness. If you have fallen in love with your married man or *are* falling in love with him, be careful—loving him is a recipe for disaster, and you are destined to get hurt (as he will *never* leave his wife for you, whatever he may be telling you). But more about that later.

🗝 **TIP FOR HOPEFUL MISTRESSES:** In order to keep it real and keep your sanity intact, always try to remind yourself that even if he did leave her for you (which he won't) and was suddenly free and available (which he won't be), you might not actually want him!

This is a very valid suggestion, ladies. He may not seem so attractive to you if the dynamics change. You might even view him as damaged goods. Sometimes when you want something so badly and wait for it to happen for so long, if it actually *does* happen, you end up asking yourself what all the fuss was about. You could feel let-down, even disappointed.

✎ **NOTE TO SELF:** Could the "mistress in waiting" actually be a victim? A victim of the old "wanting what one can't have" syndrome? But on the other hand, unless she actually gets to have him, how can she ever know if she really wanted him or not? (Damn, it's hard to stay sane.)

You wanted him so badly when he was with someone else that it was all you thought about. But if he was suddenly free, you could find yourself thinking, "Well, if his wife didn't want him, then I don't either!" (This is much more pertinent if she kicks him out and *then* he comes to you, which for the record means he didn't leave her at all!)

✎ **NOTE OF PROJECTED GUIDANCE TO MISTRESSES:** If his "Mrs." does kick him out of the proverbial home and he then comes to start a relationship with you, he is far more likely to try and snake his way back into his wife's affections in the future (whether she is officially the "ex" or his "still to become ex"). That will be his perpetual challenge. He will obviously never share this goal with you, but basically if she throws him out, you can never trust him again. (Ha! Like you could anyway? Adultery and trust must be the ultimate oxymoron!)

The information for this book took a long time to collate, and I can tell you it wasn't *all* fun. The content is true, and everything you will read has happened to somebody (you'll just never be quite sure whom).

It goes without saying that I have changed the names in the stories. The name changes are mostly to protect the men in the affair, especially the high profile ones. (Oh, okay, so you got me there. It's actually to prevent them from suing me!)

Ironically, my research showed that most mistresses do not want anonymity at all. Quite the opposite in fact, and they have been more than happy to talk to me about every detail, thrilled and even relieved they finally had an outlet to express themselves and vent their feelings.

The most common grievance was the unjustness they felt at being portrayed as the predatory villain when an affair is exposed, whilst the husband (the real predatory villain) gets away lightly, especially if he happens to be rich.

The wives of the wealthy will typically shed a few crocodile tears, insist on financial compensation for what he has done (and for the "social embarrassment" it has caused her), then revert right back to their original policy of indifference, pronto! However, "Mr. Money Bags Husband" won't care. Are you kidding me? He will be more than happy to comply with anything in order to smoothly pave his yellow brick road to future adulterous liaisons. He will click his heels and be back on "cheater's row" before you can say Dorothy *(or Monica, Jessica, or Sandra)*.

Clearly, the extramarital affair remains a hot subject. From the latest Hollywood couples splitting up because of sex with an unknown, right down to your next-door neighbor doing the same thing, we tend to listen to the cheating love-rat stories with ironic glee. We further revel in the salacious glossy magazine exposés of one half of a beautiful celebrity couple cheating on the other (and it's awesome if it happens to be with a subordinate or hired help like a nanny or personal assistant, although a waitress is equally as good). We read with hypnotic fascination. With questions like, "How could he or she possibly cheat?!" These people are so perfect, so rich, so tall, skinny, and shallow. Basically they have it all.

✎ **NOTE OF HYPOCRISY:** This brings me back to my point. Even though the topic is thrashed about and put in our faces on a daily basis, the status of actually being in an affair is still deemed socially unacceptable and not appropriate dinner conversation, especially if it involves anyone around that particular dining table. Hence, the regular Joes and Josephines involved in extramarital affairs sadly learn to keep their mouths shut when it comes to talking about themselves and their personal lives ("shhh" being the key word to an affair!).

✎ **ETIQUETTE NOTE TO ADULTEROUS DINERS:** I wouldn't worry about it too much. It's awfully rude to talk when you're eating anyway!

Most of those I interviewed welcomed learning about other women's similar situations. Some treated it as a form of group therapy. *Some as exorcism!*

During my research, I listened to volumes of real-life experiences from women and men too—both equally as interesting and surprising as the next. In fact, I really don't think much could shock me anymore.

I have met and interviewed mistresses all over the world, women of all ages and backgrounds. Many who were kind enough to share their experiences with me became my friends. Some were already friends to begin with.

✎ **NOTE TO PUBLIC:** For any innocent interviewees who didn't realize I was interrogating and analyzing you, I apologize.

I discovered that a very small percentage of men actually do leave their wives for their mistress—although it is usually as a last resort, after his wife has found out about everything and thrown him out of the house. At which point he could well turn up on your doorstep with a sports bag full of clean shirts and a collection of dirty thoughts. If that's the result you're hoping for, then I do hope you get it. However, for most mistresses, who foolishly (and pathetically) believe that he will leave his wife only to find that it never happens (just in case you had forgotten), this book is for you. It tells it as it is—bringing you face-to-face with reality (ouch!).

One of the driving forces behind this project was the huge number of adulterous relationships I have witnessed and the amount of crap I've been fed during those I have experienced personally. Ultimately, I don't have one friend (married or single, male or female) who is not currently embroiled in an affair, who hasn't had one or more affairs, or who wouldn't just plain love to have one now. LOVE TO!

Extramarital affairs are all around me. I know these stories well as I am living them daily. My material comes to me, so to follow the well-known adage that "you should write about what you know," I am!

✎ **NOTE OF MY QUALIFICATIONS TO WRITE THIS BOOK:**
I'm a single thirty-something woman—a woman who has wasted her fair share of time on affairs and who is willing to come clean about her

behavior, and his behavior, during certain liaisons. Believe me when I say I have heard it all before…*and then some!*

Because I have been a mistress, I know how a mistress feels and acts, and it is my responsibility to tell you who we really are and just how much we are compromising. I'm tired of seeing fabulous women waste themselves on bullshit affairs with cheating, insincere, cowardly losers.

✎ **NOTE OF AFFIRMATION:** Sisters, we are worth more than that, and we need to wise up. So stay with me here.

Please don't think I'm a butch lesbian (and butch lesbians, please don't take offense at that comment) or a scorned woman who totally berates men because I hate them. I am neither. I adore men—I couldn't live without them. I just know what makes them tick, that's all, and I'm not afraid to vocalize it.

I will be speaking directly to women suffering emotionally as a result of being in love with a married man, while he on the other hand is having his (New York–style cheese-) cake and eating it too. But as a mistress, you are letting him. You are enabling his infidelities. He's the horse and you're the water—he didn't need much leading, but boy was he thirsty when he arrived. (There is probably a drought over at his house!)

✎ **ASSERTIVE NOTE TO WET MISTRESSES:** Isn't it time you had a slice of the cake yourself? If this "agreement" is not benefiting you in any way (other than sex), then you are doing it all wrong. Don't you think it's a little one-sided in his favor and that you should at least focus on getting something more out of it—even if it doesn't end up being him? (Which in the bigger scheme of things could actually be a *very* lucky escape for you!)

chapter 2

The Extreme Differences Between Men and Women
Or Between How the Sisterhood and the Brotherhood Think!

 Okay, sisters, this chapter is for all of you, regardless the type of relationship you're in. And before we go any further, let's establish some of the inherent characteristics men possess (whether they're married or single).

Fundamentally, deep down (some deeper than others), men are generally selfish, scheming, self-absorbed, obstinate, devious, lying, cheating, insensitive, egotistical bastards (many with a flatulence problem). Does that sound harsh?

Most do not possess a conscience (it would just get in their way), and because the art of lying comes so naturally to them, they tend to have their own take on reality and their own versions of the truth (although, as *we* know, the truth doesn't have versions, does it!).

✎ **NOTE TO THE SISTERHOOD:** I won't list the wonderful attributes that we as the female race were lucky enough to be given, as you should know them already, but God certainly dealt us a good hand, didn't he? Things like being caring, considerate, open, and compassionate are a good place to start.

I recently heard a straight man telling a woman, "All men are dogs." Considering it came from the horse's mouth, so to speak, I feel quite within the rights of my description. If one of the brotherhood describes his own kind that way, what the hell hope do the rest of us have, eh?

✎ **NOTE TO SISTERS WHO ARE MISTRESSES:** Let us not appear to be hypocritical though, because if men weren't all the things I describe, we wouldn't be able to have an affair with them, right?

Of course, in the married man who is having an affair, these quintessential traits will be far more pronounced, particularly the lying, cheating, and devious attributes of his character.

✎ **NOTE TO SELF:** As mistresses, we don't address his character flaws at the start because it suits us to go along with it all. But as the affair travels along, we become co-dependent within it and therefore blind to what he really stands for. It's only when things go pear shaped (i.e., when we aren't getting enough of what we want) that we actually open our eyes and see him for the liar and cheat he really is...*and always has been.*

⚷ **HANDY TIP FOR ANY WIVES STILL READING:** Because these particular traits are ramped up in the husband priming himself for an affair (or in the middle of a full-blown affair), they shouldn't be too difficult for you to spot, as he will definitely be fine-tuning his unique selling points and practicing his duplicitous strengths and weaknesses, ready to pounce. You won't want to accept it at the time (and as usual you may be indifferent to the whole thing anyway).

Most intelligent women know that when women use the term "we" they are referring to themselves and their partner or significant other. When men use the word "we," they are referring to themselves and *their* significant other—their dick, to whom they always give priority and make time for. Sorry for the bluntness, but it is what it is, after all!

In my opinion, these are some of the barefaced facts and balls-up honest truths about the distinguishing qualities of men. Of course, there are always going to be some exceptions to the rule (even a broken clock is right twice a day), but I'm making a generalization here.

The *Extreme* Differences Between Men and Women
Or Between How the Sisterhood and the Brotherhood Think

By the way, if any sisters are reading this and angrily thinking I've got it "all wrong," "out of proportion," or have even "lost the plot," please, I urge you to keep on reading and then decide.

If you really doubt my observations about men, you are either in denial or in the throes of a wonderful affair or relationship. But trust me, at some point your other half (I hate that expression) will do something to embarrass you, humiliate you, or just downright piss you off. You'll find yourself reaching for this book to reread and highlight some of the points you refused to initially accept (the points you didn't think applied to *you*).

✎ **NOTE TO SISTERS:** Why do we belittle ourselves by referring to any man as our "other half"? Are we implying that if he leaves us we are only ever going to be half a person, at least until we can locate another "half" to replace him and make us whole again?

✎ **NOTE TO MISTRESSES:** A married-man lover should never be allowed to go by the title of your "other half." Please. That's just dumb! But he could perhaps go under the auspice of your "other quarter," or even your "other two percent"!

My opinion and description of men doesn't mean I think men are bad people, nor that for one minute we should dislike them for their veritable rainbow of true colors. I certainly don't mean that at all. But let's just be honest with ourselves in advance of getting involved with one of them. Let's be clear about what we're dealing with here so we can stay one step ahead of them. (Let's be real or let's not play.)

✎ **NOTE TO READERS:** From now on I will be referring to married men as "MMs" for reasons of simplicity (not that I'm inferring that men are "simple").

Now let's move on and take a look at some more male differentiae. On a positive note, they are forgetful and aren't good with details, meaning they're not as proficient at lying as they think they are (you need a good memory to be a good liar). Most are easily taken advantage of, given half the chance, and because they are not as sharp as we sisters, they often sail close to the wind and run the risk of having their affair exposed to the wife.

✎ **NOTE TO FRUSTRATED, ANGRY MISTRESSES:** That's if you don't call her first and tell her all about it...but more on that later.

Like any race, there are of course different extremes (and as I said, I am not referring to *all men)*. Most men, however, possess some, if not all, of the elements I have mentioned in varying degrees. Some may take longer than others to show that side of themselves, but by default they all will at some point.

You could find yourself in a certain situation where your other half's behavior (aargh, I still hate that term) will surprise or disappoint you, even shock you. You'll think to yourself, "Wow, I didn't think he could be like that. I thought he was different from other men." And in a flash, "Mr. Wonderful" becomes "Mr. I don't think so!"

✎ **NOTE TO THE SISTERHOOD:** When you are in the "love cocktail" stage of your relationship—when you are infatuated by him, whether he is married or not—you will always think (and convince yourself) that he is "different from the rest," that he is wonderful and not like other men at all, because that's what you want to believe. (Ringing any bells, delusional sisters?)

The main point of this chapter is to highlight the differences between our two tribes and how we think, and what better example to use than intimacy. Let's talk about romance for a minute (though in a man's world that's a little longer than it sometimes lasts) and take a run through those special, romantic evenings which we love to create.

✎ **NOTE:** I will be sharing some useful tips and shortcuts with you along the way.

When you love someone, you want to be intimate with him or her as often as humanly possible, right? You want things to be nice, and you naturally want to make your man happy so that he doesn't feel the need to look elsewhere. It's not rocket science, after all.

Think of some of the effort we put into such occasions, reveling in the opportunity to show ourselves at our best. Between the trouble we take with everything—from styling our hair and exfoliating and waxing every part of our body to preparing a brilliant three-course meal—it's a real performance! Men as usual have it easy—all they have to do is put on a clean shirt and show up with a bottle of wine (some don't even go *that* far). But we want the experience to be perfect, don't we? After all, it's a direct reflection on us and a tribute to our womanhood.

✎ **A POSITIVE NOTE ABOUT BEING A MISTRESS:** One upside to being a mistress is that time is generally on your side. He doesn't live with you, which means you have the freedom to prepare and clean up everything at your leisure. If you're the other woman, you can confidently put a little more oomph into creating a night to remember for your MM, as you know you'll be able to clean up any destruction in the kitchen and generally reorganize your place after he has gone home to his wife. Perfect!

✎ **ANOTHER POSITIVE MISTRESS NOTE:** Because he won't be sleeping over with you that night, you don't need to take the extra time required to look "naturally beautiful" for him the following morning when you don't wake up next to him, leaving you free to wear your old pajamas to bed and slap on the night cream as required. Ah…life is good!

Sisters, in general, I'm sure you'll agree that most of us enjoy creating a romantic setting for the man we love, whoever he is. Mistresses, I'm sure you will agree that we make a *particularly* conscious effort in order to ensure that we outshine his wife, in his eyes, each and every time. A mistress's goal (a mistress who wants more than just an affair with her MM) is always to entice her MM. She wants to make him desire her *more* than he desires his wife, to make him want to be in a serious relationship with her *more* than with his wife, and of course to make him want to plan to leave his wife for her.

However, the harder we try and the less he makes any positive moves, the more we rot inside, eventually turning into bitter and twisted women because we just can't understand how he couldn't want to leave his wife in order to be with us, right? (Even if he left her and we actually didn't want him in the end, it would still be nice to be able to say, "No, thank you," don't you think?)

🔑 **TIP FOR MISTRESSES:** If your MM is going to be staying over after dinner (which is rare), try to be well organized. It's only for one night, after all, so make sure that you are at your most fabulous best, your place looks immaculate, and the smells coming from the kitchen really are good enough to eat.

Obviously to pull all this off you need a certain amount of time on your hands, so if you are a working mistress (strike one!—you should focus on getting a richer MM), you may want to cheat and bring in some ready-prepared food (I don't need to tell you to pretend you cooked it, though). Don't feel bad about it. This is not lying as such; it's just classed as being "economical" with the truth *(men do it all the time)*.

🍴 **CULINARY NOTE TO MISTRESSES:** I am a firm believer of cheating in the kitchen as much as you need to. He'll probably never notice, as he'll be too busy focusing on the sex that's coming his way after dessert.

🍴 **NOTE TO PSEUDO-DOMESTIC MISTRESSES:** Be sure to throw away any incriminating food boxes, and always maintain high standards. Do not leave old fruits or wilting vegetables lying around. There should never be anything "limp" or "flat" in a good mistress's kitchen — and that goes for your MM too!

So now, if you can pull the whole production together successfully, he'll tell you that not only do you look amazing, but that you are brilliant in the kitchen, second to none in the bedroom (and you can hold an interesting, articulate conversation with anyone he chooses to introduce you to, as well). Imagine how different from his wife you must already seem to him. In fact, he "doesn't quite know how you manage it all."

🍴 **NOTE TO MEN:** It's called being a mistress! Definition: No responsibilities.

🔑 **TIP FOR MISTRESSES:** If you really are challenged in the cookery department, focus on a wholesome, filling dessert, and aim to practice some extra special sexual techniques in the bedroom afterward. He will soon forget the absence of that bouquet garni in your coq au vin, trust me.

To add to said evening's romantic atmosphere and heighten the ambience at your love nest (especially if he happens to be paying the rent on it), you will no doubt choose some soft music. You could even play your special love song, the cheesy, commercialized one that you have both agreed is "your song" (you know the one). The song that means so much to you when you are an item, that ballad with the deep (tooth-decayingly sweet), meaningful words that sum up exactly how you feel about each other.

♪ **A MUSICAL NOTE:** Good examples of songs in this genre are Whitney Houston's "I Will Always Love You," Celine Dion's "Because You Loved Me" and Savage Garden's "I Knew That I Loved You Before I Met You."

That song is so necessary, isn't it? What else would you leave with a loving message on your lover's voice mail when you are apart in order to feel closer to him (or, in a mistress's case, to try to make up after yet another argument about why he won't leave his wife!).

And yes, it's that same mother of a song that makes you want to put your head over the toilet bowl and vomit profusely each time you hear it after the relationship is over (or, even worse, makes you want to cry).

🔑 **TIP FOR ALL SISTERS:** When a relationship is over, throw that stupid CD away. And if your "special" song comes on the radio, turn the damned thing off. Don't torture yourself, because here's the thing—it never, ever meant anything to him anyway. He will have suffered it all as sentimental claptrap, which as we know "men don't do"—not unless they fake it in order to guarantee having sex with you (at which point we get to fake it right back!).

After all this talk of the preparations, let's get down to business and the end result of the evening, which the man really wants to achieve—the subject of making love. I know, I know. I'm being fanciful with my terminology here, as to them it is just sex, but we have to live in hope that sex might mean more than *just* ejaculation to some men!

Let's look at the term "making love" and the facts relating to why men and women see it so differently.

Women often shamefully believe that when they are taking care of business in bed with their man (whether married or single), they are actually "making love." Granted, we accept that it usually means more to us than it does to him, but *still*. And the depth of emotion you feel is hardly surprising, is it? Especially when you have gone to such lengths (and knocked yourself out in the process) to set the scene for a perfect evening together. That in itself is a statement of just how much you care for him.

I mean, by now your place is looking like a little love palace. You've lit some beautiful-smelling long-burning candles and opened that expensive bottle of wine you were saving for a really special occasion. On top of that, you are looking absolutely killer...

✎ **NOTE:** Women having an affair with an MM usually want to appear to be more than their best when "playing house" on these occasions because they are, quite literally, *constantly* in competition with another woman—the one he already lives with. At least that's how mistresses see it. The truth is that he never compares you with her.

🔑 **TIP FOR MISTRESSES:** Never become sluggish in your appearance. For example, you don't want to open the door to greet him wearing those awful secret baggy velour sweatpants and old slippers. He gets that at home. Be sure to stay in a class of your own, and remind him of what he doesn't get!

So the scene is set, and if you have laid on the full pleasure package, not only will you be playing your special song as he walks through the door, you will have the lighting at the perfect level (to show you at your best, of course), and you will be wearing little else but his favorite body lotion and perfume. Does this sound familiar?

🖋 **NOTE TO NEW MISTRESSES WHO *ARE* BEING CONSIDERATE:** Be careful not to drown yourself in strong perfume as it may wake his wife from her deep sleep when he rolls home and throws his shirt over the bedroom chair later that evening. Better to use some light aromatherapy body oil, which will evaporate into your skin.

🖋 **NOTE TO MISTRESSES WHO *ARE NOT* BEING CONSIDERATE:** Liberally apply the strongest smelling perfume you can find all over yourself and on everything he touches (and spray a tad on his suit jacket while he's not looking, just to be sure). Calvin Klein's Obsession is always a sure bet, as is Poison by Christian Dior (both rather apt names too, huh?).

🗝 **TIP:** Try to smudge some bright-red lipstick on his shirt collar, too!

You will be sporting your best underwear and will have spent hours on "looking natural" whilst having everything ready to go—all at the same time. It's not easy. In fact it's a real production, but it's worth it, right? WRONG!

🏳 **BIG RED FLAG NOTE TO SISTERS AND MISTRESSES ALIKE:** Don't bother wasting your time, energy, and money, because you know what? He has a totally different concept of the whole event. Remember, he doesn't possess the sensitivity genes required to even come close to seeing things the way you do.

Let's be real: All he wants to do is have sex with you, so work backward from that. The music will get on his nerves (he'd rather have sports on the TV), and he's thinking that the wine tastes like a cheap, rough vino you picked up on sale at the store. With regards to the three-course meal you have so lovingly prepared, he would be just as (or more) impressed with Indian takeout, or Chinese, or both. The candles smell too girlie and are getting up his nose, and he is praying you will hurry up with the whole dinner-serving performance so he can have sex with you and still have time to make it over to the bar where his mates are, in time for last call (and to talk about real stuff!).

Many men will do anything to avoid using the term making love when it comes to having sex, because to them it adds a whole new scary dimension to how and where the goalposts of the relationship stand *(and I use the R-word loosely)*.

✎ **NOTE OF APPREHENSION:** I would like to say that "most men" avoid the term making love, but I know I will get hate mail for it (or even hate *male?*), perhaps even some from women with shattered illusions too.

Whatever the term being used, at the end of the day, a male's and a female's destination and end result are the same—their journeys are just miles apart.

If a male uses the term making love, he will be anxious that it might imply that the "event" and the union taking place is more serious that it really is. In other words, that you mean more to him than you actually do.

If he is single (not an MM), he'll worry that the term making love will have you thinking he is your monogamous boyfriend in no time at all, followed by talk of marriage, babies, and mortgages.

If he is married, he'll worry that as a mistress you could start to get ideas above your station (it happens, you know) and anticipate him leaving his wife for you.

✎ **A REAL QUOTE NOTE FROM AN MM:** "Men just can't use *that term* with women, especially if it's a casual thing, because as soon as they do, she automatically thinks it is more than *just sex.* It can kill the whole mood." *(Bless!)*

For the record, this MM happened to be over three hundred pounds with a heavily pregnant wife sitting at home waiting for him, leaving me thinking, "Wow, who in their right mind would ever sleep with you, period? But more to the point, where in the hell do you get your attitude from? I mean, have you looked in the mirror?" YUCK!

Men are soooo self-absorbed that sometimes it's scary. But that was this man's take on the term making love, and sadly I think he was speaking for many of his tribe.

It's a similar situation with the statement "I love you." If he does tell you that on a regular basis, he may not say it with quite the same pizzazz while you are having sex as he does on another occasions. (And note that an "I love you" when you have cooked his favorite meal to perfection, for example, is way different to an "I love you" said in the sack.)

✎ **NOTE TO SISTERS:** The terms "I love you" and "I love ya" have very, very different meanings, so be sure to listen carefully. "I love ya" doesn't count for anything in a relationship (other than it's quite a nice thing to say to people you genuinely like), but it *can* be used to placate many a "selective hearing" female when a man finds himself in a tight spot: "You know I love ya" said at the right moment can often buy him a bit of valuable time and sexual gratification.

My description in this chapter gives a sort of clarity to the subject of men, doesn't it? Lord knows they think enough tripe about us—melodramatic, nagging, demanding, "bunny boilers" all spring to mind. If only they had enough sense to realize that if we *do* display any of those tendencies, it is usually as backlash against all the crapola they feed us.

If you can't get your head around all men being dogs, read on a little and you soon will. If you still don't think so by the end of this book, then write to my agent and he'll refund you *double* the amount you paid. (Just kidding!)

✎ **NOTE TO SKEPTICAL SISTERS:** Just in case you are wavering in your thought process, let me leave you with two of the most important C-words that are used in any relationship, along with the definitions of them (as perceived by men and by women):

COMMITMENT

FEMALE DEFINITION: A desire to get married and raise a family with that special person.
MALE DEFINITION: Trying not to hit on other women while out with the current one.

COMMUNICATION

FEMALE DEFINITION: The open sharing of thoughts and feelings with one's partner.
MALE DEFINITION: Leaving a note on the fridge door before taking off on a golfing trip with the boys.

chapter 3

How and Why Married Men Stray

And Why Their Wives Stay

 Marriage can be viewed as a blessing (although some may consider it a death sentence), and it is one of the hardest challenges that any two consenting adults can ever enter into. People get married for all sorts of reasons—the most pertinent one, hopefully, is love.

✎ **NOTE:** Love can sometimes be confused with *lust*, an easy mistake to make, especially as they both begin with the same letter.

Like most things, love fades once it becomes the norm, after that first frisson of excitement has worn off. The feelings and reasons that sparked the initial love relationship are often forgotten when partners start taking each other for granted, especially when the added stress of kids, family, and work life are thrown into the mix. They can become too familiar and too complacent with each other, and there is no challenge left. Rather than work at what's actually wrong in the relationship, many people find it easier to let things go *(enter here: the perfect setting for an affair)*.

✎ **FACTUAL NOTE:** A man who cheats on his wife leaves his marital relationship, mentally and emotionally, long before he leaves it sexually, as the most important sexual organ in his body is actually what lies between his ears, *not* between his hips! So if his wife isn't stimulating his brain, he will actively seek out someone who does. The sex will automatically follow.

Marriage can soon become a boring way of life, seemingly full of nothing but responsibilities and obligations.

Men and women typically get married because: a) she is pregnant or b) they think it's what they want when they are young and just starting out in life (especially men, as they need a woman to look after them and their laundry/meal requirements when they move out of their mother's house).

People don't want to be alone in life, so marriage is a natural transition, especially when all one's peers are doing the same thing. However, it becomes a far more demanding business than when they were just at the "relationship stage," before that terribly *serious* stuff of taking vows and making promises to each other. That time when the two participants attach themselves to the ball and chain (which in the future could become known as alimony), and surrender their lives to monogamy and monotony until death comes to part them (a welcome release in some cases!).

✎ **INTERESTING NOTE:** Ironically, the reasons two people chose to get married in the first place often end up becoming the paradoxical precursor for an affair.

However, if the marriage is a healthy one made up of two people who love and respect each other and go out of their way to make a success of their union, then the marriage *should* grow and become stronger as the individuals within it grow together instead of apart.

If this is your situation, then this book isn't for you, but I congratulate you and wish you great happiness in your lives together. You are proof that it *is* possible to meet the right life partner (commonly referred to as a *soul mate*) and to live a happy, fully satisfying existence without the desire to cheat. It just doesn't happen often, that's all!

✎ **OBSERVATIONAL NOTE:** How many marriages do you see that you honestly admire? And how many married people do you ever hear say, "I have the greatest relationship in the world. *I'm so happy.*"

The world is full of married men. Many of them are unhappily married, or at least on the lookout for a willing female distraction as often as they can get away with it.

Let me make it clear once more that I am not talking about *all* men, *just most*. If this offends you, scares you, or depresses you, then I suggest you stop reading now. Because believe me, it's going to get a lot worse as I start examining the traits I suggested men possess in the previous chapter.

With regards to statistics on adultery, given the inherent secrecy, it's tough to get a true handle on how many of us are having affairs, although up to thirty-seven percent of men and twenty-two percent of women admit to it. Researchers believe that the vast majority of the millions of people who visit chat rooms have multiple "special friends," although *DivorceMag* reported that only forty-six percent of men believe online affairs are adultery. (That statistic was as surprising to me as discovering that there is a magazine dedicated purely to divorce!)

Because people have their own version of what they "think" is cheating, true figures are hard to find. A 1998 report from a study carried out by the University of California–San Francisco showed that about twenty-four percent of men and fourteen percent of women have had sex outside their marriages (and it is widely known that two-thirds of marriages in Southern California end in divorce). But my personal favorite is the lesser-known fact that those cheaters who *do* actually divorce rarely marry the person with whom they had the affair. In fact, Dr. Jan Halper's study of successful men (executives, entrepreneurs, and professionals) found that only a measly three percent of the 4,100 men surveyed eventually married their lovers.

✎ **FAIRLY-SAFE-BET-OF-A-STATISTIC NOTE:** Dr. Alfred Kinsey, the American human biologist who started a sexual revolution in the 1940s and 1950s and who was viewed as a sex guru in his time, carried out a survey revealing that sixty percent of men and forty percent of women would have an extramarital affair during their lifetime.

These figures seem to be consistent with all of the research I've carried out, so I am going to stick with Dr. K. and his findings (especially since the ever-sexy Liam Neeson played him so well in the 2004 movie about his life).

Regardless of whatever the surveys, reports, and investigations find, the truest statistics are usually closer to home. Just look around you. Take a look at how many people from your circle of friends, acquaintances, and coworkers (not to mention yourself), are in an affair, or have told you they've had one, or just speculate that they would be up for having one.

The subject of marriage—and in particular why men cheat—can open a whole other discussion on commitment issues. Like are we *really* put on this earth to be with just one person for the rest of our lives, and is that healthy? I mean, as human beings we don't do any one thing for our entire lives, do we? Most of us don't plan to only have one job, one house, one holiday destination, or, God forbid, one pair of shoes.

Society pushes us to have more and more of everything, even if we can't afford it, as though possessions define our status in life.

✎ **NOTE:** This is much like the "rich playboy" category of adulterous MMs, whose "must have" list includes a gorgeous modelesque mistress on his arm with whom, by association, he is able to parade his wealth and success. It's his statement to the outside world.

I tend to liken relationships to the "one pair of shoes" analogy, as it seems to hit home so well. Imagine only having one pair of shoes throughout your entire adult life. How awful would that be? Not only will those shoes get worn out, but you'll also get bored with them, take them for granted, end up hating them, and eventually want to try others, dumping those in the process (and yes, *even if they have been good to you*).

If you are a wife reading this (and I *did* advise you to stop!), be assured that I am not likening *you* to a pair of shoes. Although by now, you're more than likely enraged, worried, or just open to hearing more (perhaps all three). My guess is that you'll be checking your husband's credit card bills and shirt collars more thoroughly than usual when he gets home tonight (that is, if you've actually stayed up late enough to see him, of course).

So one of the main reasons that MMs cheat on their wives is down to the male ego and the low boredom threshold they possess. It's part of the "one pair of shoes syndrome" along with (yes, you know what's coming) the infamous "my wife doesn't understand me" line.

✎ **A RULE-OF-THUMB NOTE:** After a husband cheats once, it becomes easier for him to do it again and again, dealing with the guilt more and more successfully each time and gradually making it a way of life. It's not easy to live such a duplicitous life, though, and he'll need a good memory to keep track of his lies.

Those who married young, maybe as students, aspired to find success in their lives and looked forward to it, but sometimes when it comes, it can also be the reason for a marriage to deteriorate. Think about it. The husband lands a high-powered job involving traveling the world or micromanaging hundreds of people while his wife stays at home managing a family and a four-bedroom house.

In theory it should work because that's the goal they were working toward, right? That's the ideal picture of life that is painted and ingrained in us by society. In practice, however, the husband will probably find his busy (velour sweatsuit-clad) housewife becoming tired and impatient from juggling her domestic duties, school runs, and the multiple meals she has to cook.

✎ **NOTE TO MEN:** We can't all look like Nigella Lawson in the kitchen, you know!

The wife will no longer be the insatiable love kitten who used to open the door wearing nothing but sexy lingerie. Now she may not even have the interest or time to come to the door at all!

Sadly, many suburban housewives tend to pile on the pounds when they get married, and after a few kids they could likely be sporting prominent stretch marks along with breasts that are headed south.

This can be hard to take for the MM who tries to keep himself healthy and in shape, and even worse for the MM with money.

No rich, successful guy wants a fat, sloppy wife. It's a bad reflection on his success. He should be seen as the man with the best of everything, the man continually trading up and doing well (enter here: the hot young mistress).

But men can't upgrade in the women stakes without money, which is why a lot of financially challenged men "settle" for getting (or staying) married. It is often a far better option for a regular working-class guy to pool his resources with someone else—especially if he doesn't have much to pool to begin with. Starting with zero, he has nothing to lose.

A man once told me that many men view women in the same way as a cheap suit. No man *wants* to wear a cheap, off-the-peg suit by choice, but sometimes he has to if that's the best he can afford at the time—the best he can have in his circumstances. He might have to wear that knock-off, "own label," ill-fitting attire until he can afford better.

A lot of men may have married a cheap, shiny suit and were happy with it at the time, felt comfortable in it. But if their circumstances drastically improved and they have progressed up the ladder of life as successful businessmen, they could be looking to replace her with an expensive designer-label version to go with their new image.

If this newly successful man has gone on to become *really* successful, perhaps he'll be looking at a custom-made, tailored number, coupled with a monogrammed handmade shirt.

✎ **NOTE:** Ladies, I know that's a bizarre comparison, but it hits it home about how men see their wives—and women in general. They see them as an important accessory, just as they do their clothing. I'm not wrong in this; for many men it's all about getting their image right to the outside world.

The same comparison could be made to cars. A man will drive a rusty old Honda Civic only if he truly *has* to, but if he makes it big in life, he'll be looking to upgrade to the top-of-the-line BMW as soon as he can (many with secret, inbred, even *constipated* aspirations for a Ferrari one day).

✎ **NOTE:** Of course, there will be those men who ultimately drive rusty old Honda Civics and wear cheap suits all their lives. They do not feature in my research for obvious reasons, and if they're able even to get a wife, let alone a mistress, good luck to them (and more fool her!).

So then, if we take the first, most common example of married life, you will see how the goalposts can change hugely from the day one says "I do" to the reality of the man going to work and the woman staying at home and looking after his children.

✎ **NOTE:** For all of you politically correct readers, I recognize that the wife can land a high-powered job too and that everything I'm writing here could be reversed. But for the purpose of this book, we are examining married men, not married women. You know that already!

Mistresses, another reason your MM may give for straying—*with you*—could be that he "only married his wife because she got pregnant." He never would've ended up with her otherwise. He didn't love her and even on his wedding day wanted to back out. But they were young, and he felt it was the right thing to do for all concerned so that the child didn't grow up in a broken home—implying that he was forced and compromised, never intending to be faithful nor together forever at all. I wonder if the bride, *with child,* knew that on her special day?

✎ **NOTE TO MISTRESSES:** This is a frequently used reason, and I'm not suggesting that he is lying (heaven forbid!), but sadly many cheating MMs in this category will still be telling themselves this excuse—and you, if you hang around too long—twenty years into their marriage, well *after* the kid has gone to university. He actually could've done something about it if he'd really wanted to, but he was just too complacent.

Another scenario could be that the wife was equally (or even more) successful than her husband, pre-marriage and kids. This would help immensely in her daily duty of holding articulate, lively evening discussions with her husband when he got in from work, remembering to ask about how *his day* at the office was. (Note the *self-absorbed* attribute here, with which he will expect to be indulged when he graces the family abode.)

But her success may also end up being used to her detriment; she could feel cheated by having given up a high flying career to endure such a change in lifestyle while her husband is "having it all," causing tension at home and the need for *him* to seek emotional release outside (potential mistresses, prepare to be on standby).

The usual argument ensues: "Why don't you spend more time at home with me and the kids?" Why? Because it's boring for him, that's why! He knows he can have that any time he wants, so he'd rather be out trying to get what he *can't have,* like the hot new girl who works in personnel—you know, the young blonde with great legs, the one who doesn't nag him all the time.

He wants to be at the bar with his mates, playing golf, or perhaps seeing his *other* woman. (Note the *selfish* attribute rearing its head.) The first two activities may be used as his excuses to actually carry out the third activity. (Note the *devious* attribute. This one seems to come as second nature to most men.)

A lot of wives go back to work when the kids are old enough, but the damage caused by her husband's wandering eye is often done by then, especially as she becomes *more* busy trying to juggle work, kids, *and* HIM. She also may have hung on to some of that "junk in the trunk" weight that stay-at-home wives tend to gain and find hard to shake off. This can be incredibly off-putting to a cheating husband who feels he can get better and *deserves* better (one who will stray until he finds it!).

✎ **NOTE:** The irony of this is that the less attention he shows toward his wife, the less she will care about her weight and her appearance. Marital sex will typically become a "lights off" mercy/guilt trip event of the missionary kind!

The MM may start staying late at the office to avoid the hectic meal and bathtime experience at home (this applies where young kids are involved), leaving him less time to interact with his wife. These days they have very little in common anyway.

If husband and wife have developed at different rates (i.e., if through his career he has developed at a sharper pace than she has), he may want to stay late at the office to be in the company of his "like-minded" colleagues and friends—people who are on the same page as him. Or perhaps he might prefer being in the company of a certain woman, one who *does* open the door for him wearing sexy lingerie. If she happens to work at the same company as he does, it will be perfect for him both time-wise and excuse-wise. And it also provides a healthy, never-ending wealth of conversation, sexual energy, and flirtation between the two of them.

✎ **NOTE TO MISTRESSES IN THE WORKPLACE:** The risk of being found out is always exciting—plus you get to dress in your best and impress him on a daily basis. However, if you do work with him and the affair ends badly, it has the potential to be disastrous for all concerned (especially for him if you become bitter!).

If it's a work affair and the MM's mistress happens to be a subordinate to him, he will be in seventh heaven. Think of all that constant adoration he will get from her on a daily basis. The sucking up to him and ass kissing (no pun intended) that comes with the territory—by default of her subordinate position—will make him feel like he owns the world.

This will result in his sexual needs being well taken care of during office hours. *Perfect!* (Note the *egotistical* attribute being used at its best here.) He won't have to cover his back so much at home with extra lies and alibis, nor make the extra time normally required for an affair outside regular office hours.

✎ **NOTE TO WIVES:** The MM embroiled in an office affair is actually doing his wife a favor in the long run, as he won't need to take huge chunks of time outside the workplace in order to conduct adulterous liaisons, time that could be spent with her and the kids. Thus he can still be at home at a reasonable hour and give the kids a quick kiss goodnight before they go to bed. (A good example of how thoughtful a cheating MM can be when you *least* expect it.)

To sum up, if the MM's affair is work-based, he can comfortably mix the adultery and cheating to suit his ego (along with daily sexual gratification), and it will *ease* the pressure on him to lie to his wife. I say *ease* because, when he does use the excuse that he's working late at the office, or off on a business trip somewhere (accompanied by his mistress), he isn't actually lying.

A work affair makes things easier for the MM in general and gives him less guilt to carry around in his already busy day. After all, he is only being "economical" with the truth and choosing to leave out certain details that would just make his wife worry (and God knows she already has enough to do being such a wonderful mother to his children).

The excuses he gives to his wife about not being home for dinner because he is held up at the office, and so on, may actually wash with her. To be fair, he could well be stuck there late into the evening; it just depends whether she would agree that having sex with his mistress on the Xerox machine or wining and dining her on the company card (so his wife doesn't see the bill) falls under the category of "working late." She may not see it in quite the same light as he does, especially when she is trying to get his children to sleep or their homework done, while she is grabbing a sandwich on the go. (As I said, these are just annoying little details that he quite rightly shouldn't burden her with. It's not fair to her!)

✎ **HELPFUL NOTE TO (SUSPECTING) WIVES:** If your husband is supposedly working overtime, how come it doesn't show up on his paycheck? And have you ever found out by accident that he took a vacation day but supposedly worked that day? Go with your intuition—in these instances, it will usually be right.

Let's get back to those business trips, the ones that will become more frequent if he is having an affair. He *is* physically where he said he would be and has even given his wife the name and number of the hotel he's staying in. So he *must* be alone, and everything is kosher, right?

Wrong.

The truth is that the mistress has signed in at the reception desk as *Mrs. Cheater* (for want of a better name). She would've had to sign in by law as the hotel needs to know how many people are there for safety reasons. So Mr. and Mrs. Cheater have been issued two room keys and voilá, they're good to go.

If the MM's wife *does* choose to call his room, that's okay, no sweat there, as he'll have it all planned out. His mistress will be used to lying next to him and providing some sexual gratification and release whilst he has to listen to his "other half" hundreds of miles away banging on about what the kids did at school that day and how he doesn't spend enough time at home. (Yak yak yakkity yak.)

✎ **NOTE TO MISTRESSES:** Some MMs may banish you to the bathroom or even the hotel balcony while he makes or takes the "wife call." It's on you whether you allow that to happen, and it goes without saying that if it is the balcony, do make sure that you're in a hot climate (and if you're not, *why not?* Hello!).

To eliminate any doubt that men are dogs, I hope that this next and final example will solidify it for you. I was talking to an unhappily married male friend of mine recently, whom I know plays around. I asked him straight out, "If your wife asked you if you were sleeping around, would you tell her the truth?"

He thought for a minute and replied, quite chagrined, "But I'm *not!* I haven't had sex with anyone."

"Oh," I said, a little perplexed. "What about the girl you took on a date last week? The sexy little Spanish one?"

His eyes lit up. "Oooh yes, her. She was grrreat!" he replied. "We ended up back at her place. I saw her naked and gave her oral sex, but I didn't *sleep* with her."

✎ **NOTE TO ALL:** Are you getting my point now? *Their* version of the truth.

Picture that scene as he saw it. Then think about how his wife would translate his infidelities upon finding out, perhaps in a conversation with her best friend.

We know it would go something like: *"Oh my God!* I just found out my bastard of a husband is playing around. He has been lying to me, cheating on me, *and* spending our money on taking other women out!"

But if we go along with how my male perpetrator friend sees it, she might say something like, "Oh, hell! You know what? I just found out, silly me, that my husband is having oral sex with a cute young girl behind my back, but what the heck. It's only oral, so I don't mind. Oral doesn't count, does it? And it doesn't mean he doesn't love me anymore, does it?"

In the same vein, I wonder what Hillary would have said to Bill had she walked in on his dirty deed in the Oval Office. "Oh, darling, I can see you're busy right now, but are you sure this is only foreplay and not sexual relations? If so, then go ahead and enjoy, and I'll have a lovely dinner waiting for you upstairs when you're finished!" "Oh, and, hi Monica. I'm sorry…I didn't recognize you from that angle, and I certainly didn't know you smoked cigars! No, no—please don't get up on my account, but do pop up and join us for dinner afterward if you'd like."

Like *hell* Hillary would've said that! Actually Clinton summed it up best when asked why he did what he did: "Because I could."

So we've looked at some of the reasons why men stray, but how about why wives stay, when they know their husband is having an affair or has had an affair? It really is quite simple, and like any form of abuse or betrayal, it falls under the category of co-dependency.

The longer the wife is married to the adulterer in question, and depending on what type of routine home life they have, she may well have gradually lost her identity along the way. The typical stay-at-home wife, whose biggest form of escapism is looking after the kids and hearing about her husband's exotic business trips, is the *most* co-dependent kind.

Think about it. He actually provides her with her identity. Being *his* wife, running the house, and existing in their joint social circle is what defines her and her life. Now throw into the mix the fact that he may be wealthy, and that adds another element of power. She literally relinquishes to him the control to direct her life, and in return he gives her an existence and an identity.

If he is exposed for having an affair, the typical stay-at-home wife will be far more likely to forgive him, and as with any form of emotional abuse, the co-dependent wife who is being hurt will always think the abuser, her husband, will reform and not do it again.

The husband, upon being exposed, may also typically manipulate her into believing that *she* is the one at fault, that he cheated because she is lacking in some way. Those wives with already low self-esteem will further believe him, and therefore stay in the relationship in order to try and right *their* wrongs.

The other end of the scale is the wife who is not in love with her husband but coexists in their relationship as it suits her, just as much as it suits him, *not* to address their issues and get out of it. She doesn't give a rat's ass what he does or who he does it with, just as long as it's not her and as long as her little apple cart isn't upset (she may be having her own affair too). On a related note, there is the society wife married to the wealthy cheater who is not going to let a fling with some floozy upset *her* lifestyle for one minute—nor her bank account and her high echelon social circle.

✎ **NOTE OF PITY:** Possibly the worst reason for a wife to stay with a known adulterer is because she is stupid and doesn't know any better, which in truth means she is more to be pitied than blamed and will be a victim all her life.

Of course, the final theory is based on that wonderfully true saying: "Misery loves company." For some couples, living in a train wreck of a relationship defines them both. It is all they know. Maybe they couldn't live without the drama, rejection, and self-pity they both endure from each other daily. *Maybe they just forgot how to be happy!*

☛ **STERN NOTE OF WARNING TO MISTRESSES:** The MM who cheats is ultimately holding everyone involved in his triangle of deceit as a hostage, including himself. If you're not careful, your emotions may eventually end up being used as ransom for his cowardliness.

chapter 4

Single, Female, and Desperate?

Why Single Women Opt to Date Married Men

 Before I get to the reasons why single, vivacious, fabulous women choose to resort to affairs with married men, let's take a look at the whole big picture about why women are increasingly single later in life.

These days, if you're a woman in your mid-thirties and upward, and still single (although I prefer to call it unmarried because single implies that you're just *waiting* to get married), people automatically seem to feel sorry for you, inquiring in hushed tones as to why. In other words, "What's wrong with you?"

✎ **NOTE OF REFERENCE:** I will be referring to "single unmarried women" (which I'm proud to say I am) as SUWs from now on—not to be confused with SUVs, of course. Although when you think of it, *both* can provide a little off-terrain weekend activity if treated properly and not handled too roughly.

People, especially older people, generally assume there's something "wrong" if you can't get a man—i.e., if you are an SUW. Their thoughts are, "Why aren't you married at the ripe old age of thirty-five?" Or, "When are you going to have kids?" They never say, "Ooh, yes, you are such a wonderful woman, a real catch, and with so much to offer. I can see *exactly* why you choose to remain single based on the pure flotsam of men that seems to be currently floating around out there" (further agreeing with you wholeheartedly that you shouldn't settle for second best!).

🖋 **NOTE TO SUWs:** Wouldn't it be refreshing to hear that said? Just occasionally?

Many of you may be familiar with a front-page article that appeared in *Newsweek* magazine back in 1986 stating that a forty-year-old, single, white, college-educated woman was more likely to be killed by a terrorist than to marry.

Obviously the article was written pre-9/11—it is now a politically incorrect example (if it ever was okay), and I'm sure the wording has come back to haunt someone. But *Newsweek* obviously wanted to make a point and stir up a reaction. Apparently it did.

What that statement shows is that even some twenty years ago, many of the same "single women syndromes" must have been out there. There must have been enough evidence to back up such a statement within that article.

It evoked the reaction the magazine sought, and women all over the U.S. were up in arms, fueled by fury, anxiety, and skepticism. Yes, it was a shocking statement. There is no denying that. But at the same time, an element of truth probably lodged itself in many a single woman's psyche (if not in her throat too!).

🖋 **NOTE OF HOPE TO SISTERS:** In the same article, *Newsweek* gave thirty-five-year-old women a whopping five percent chance of getting married. Gee, thanks!

Interestingly enough, there is never the same amount of research into the reasons behind the statistics; why there were—and are—so many thirty- to forty-year-old SUWs out there in the first place. So let's do our own research and take a look at some possible theories behind such sweeping statements. Let's look at why fabulous women in their prime are choosing to live as singletons, or alternatively succumbing to dead-end affairs with married men.

Single, Female, and Desperate?
Why Single Women Opt to Date Married Men

Reason number one would have to be the severe shortage—in fact, a veritable drought—of available single men in today's marketplace (and even fewer that would qualify for the job of being marriage material).

✎ **PERSONAL OPINION NOTE:** I would suggest that the reason this fact isn't investigated and publicized is because "startling statistics" sell newspapers and magazines. It's far more salacious and in keeping with public appetite and negative opinion to suggest that women are the ones at fault and totally inept at securing a husband.

Intelligent, career-minded women might as well have bubonic plague the way they are sometimes berated for putting more effort into carving out a healthy career for themselves than into marriage and babies. Anyone ever wondered why? Could it possibly have anything to do with the fact that women now realize that the days of eligible bachelors queuing up to marry them are long gone? Women these days have come to terms with the fact that they can no longer rely on the old-fashioned fairy-tale picture of a man supporting his wife while housed in a white picket-fenced cottage with red roses around the door.

✎ **NOTE:** SUWs are so tired of "looking" and coming across losers that, quite frankly, even if Prince Charming *did* come along, we probably wouldn't even recognize him and would dismiss him along with the rest of the flotsam out there. This could be due to us looking at life with a flawed perspective (i.e., as a mistress?).

Therefore, many of us SUWs are faced with very real fears and are left little choice but to structure our career as a way of securing our own future and facilitating our own standard of lifestyle, resigning ourselves to the fact that we may never meet our life partner.

✎ **NOTE:** We also need to know that we have enough money set aside to pay for sperm donation and single motherhood, which we might feel we need when we turn forty and find we're still SUWs, as we're not all the Angelina Jolies of the child-adopting world, are we?

Though on that note, it is damned annoying to think that a single woman who wants to have a baby has to *pay* for a man's sperm when we all know that there is so much of it out there going to waste. (Men get paid a handsome amount for donating their sperm, by the way).

✎ **NOTE TO SISTERS:** What a perfect job for some guys—being a wanker for a living! Ha!

But these savings will never go to waste, as even if an SUW eventually marries in her forties, she can put the "sperm fund" money to good use on the IVF treatment she will undoubtedly need to become pregnant (penance for leaving reproduction so late in life). If she should happen to conceive naturally with her new husband, then she can always put the sperm savings toward a fancy new leather sofa.

Now, back to that article. Let's bear in mind that such controversial subject matter was put out there in the mid-eighties, pre the *Sex and the City* days and before the groundbreaking and somewhat addictive discovery of online dating.

There was no Ally McBeal or Bridget Jones to resonate with whilst downing bottles of chardonnay and comparing one's woeful single life to TV characters. There were absolutely no reality TV shows that promised to find women a blind date, a bachelor, or a father for their children. So how in the hell, one wonders, did these young women cope without such shows to escape into and without which to validate their singleton plight in life?

An interesting survey would be whether the same demographic of single women in 2006 are any better off than they were twenty years ago—and if they have learned anything along the way.

Just because we talk the subject to death and make hit TV shows, books, and movies out of it, doesn't mean we're any closer to understanding the enigma of love and marriage. (Although it is definitely more acceptable, even quite fashionable, to be single nowadays.)

My personal take on being an SUW is that I'm not unhappy being single—truly I'm not—and it does have its good points. I would honestly much rather be single than compromise by being with a man who wasn't "the one"—the one I had been looking thirty-six long years for anyway—just so I could fit into society by getting married and having all the trappings, like a Mercedes in the driveway and a supermarket rewards card in my wallet. However, at the same time, *of course* I want that wonderful man that will be my soul mate with whom I will have innate chemistry and constant sexual desire, who will totally "get" me, who will help me grow as we grow together, who will be faithful to me, with whom I will have a successful, prosperous life built upon team-work and joint goals, and with whom I will enjoy sultry glasses of fine red wine on balmy evenings, watching the waves crash against the sunset from the balcony of our dream beach house in Malibu (which doesn't have a mortgage), reveling in each other's very being and set against the evocative backdrop of the Pacific Ocean.

✎ **A BACK-TO-REALITY NOTE TO SELF:** Where in God's name am I gonna find all that in one male heterosexual, eh? See what I mean about one's standards getting higher as one gets older?

The actual reality of that story will probably be more like *me* trying to make enough money to facilitate all of the above on my own, and the closest I will ever get to the ocean will be surfing the Match.com website for boy-toys who want to date successful, but washed-up, authors. Now look who's being the flotsam!

✎ **NOTE:** Do you see the depressing reality for SUWs if we allow ourselves to dream too big without any results? And do you also see why the chardonnay comes in so damned useful at times?

The *Newsweek* article was written as if to make an attack on the single woman's independence, as though we are SUWs by choice rather than circumstance, and it annoyingly resonates with most—if not all—SUWs as to why some of us just can't find that special someone (whilst others seem to).

Just where is that handsome soul mate? The one who's allegedly "out there," waiting to pick us up in his flashy new sports car or take us for romantic walks on the beach followed by cocktails at sunset.

(Oh Lord, forgive me. That sounded like a Match.com profile. Note to self: Must get out more!)

If we didn't have to keep seeing such damning articles and statistics about the number of SUWs wandering about on the loose, we wouldn't keep questioning it! We could just get on with our lives in peace. But because it's in our face almost every day in some shape or form, we have to deal with it, stress over it…and drink copious amounts of alcohol to blank it all out.

✎ **INQUIRING NOTE TO SELF:** I wonder if Bridget Jones has enrolled in AA yet or whether her liver just gave up altogether?

We do our best to deal with singledom in the face of adversity, but at the same time, we would love for a guy to sweep us off our feet and turn our heads—and any other part of our body—wouldn't we? We'd LOVE, LOVE, LOVE it! But because we wait so long, our levels of expectation are greater and our tastes more discerning, thereby making it somewhat impossible to meet the male creatures we seek—and if we do find them, they're already married or have boyfriends of their own!

So what are we supposed to do, sisters? Settle for second best just because we know our fertility clock is ticking away? Give in to family pressures to reproduce, even if we know the man we're with isn't Mr. Right? Or should we just alleviate the pressure and the singledom boredom by having an affair with that married man who is coming on to us? (The one who won't take no for an answer.)

How about this for a statistic? In 2004, the Office of National Statistics revealed that there were almost 400,000 more single men in their thirties than single women. I don't see that being broadcast on the front of *Newsweek*. It also stated that there were twice as many men in this age group living alone as there were women. Interesting, huh?

So who—and where—are these single men? Perhaps these guys don't even want a relationship or are incapable of having one (neither being an attractive scenario).

✎ **NOTE TO SISTERS:** I don't know about you, but if I meet a man over forty years old who has never been married, I find it a little disturbing and I question it. (Maybe men do the same with SUWs.) I also don't particularly want a guy who has been married and has kids, and has therefore "done it all" before, but realistically I know I would have to settle for one. Aargh, it's so hard out there for an SUW!

It would be very refreshing to see a survey on why these men are single. Perhaps they blame their laziness (in trying to meet our "high" standards?) for their seemingly eternal single status.

✎ **NOTE TO ALL SUW SISTERS:** Perhaps we have met some of these older single men and found them hideously boring, or maybe these "available" men are in bed with each other (if you happen to believe some of the gay statistics out there). Perhaps we single sisters are the new bachelors?

My research showed that the more independent and successful we SUWs become—by default of being single—the type of man we are attracted to is the powerful businessman, the man who has huge confidence and presence about him, who commands attention by his very persona when he walks in a room (think of President Bill Clinton, for example).

These men are, of course, already married (think of Clinton again). But if they are the ones who come on to us and fit the profile of what we think we're looking for and need in our lives, we go ahead with it, married or not! (Um, Clinton AGAIN.)

Whatever the reason, the bottom line is that many women have grown to have far lower requirements for men and their place in our lives. They are hardly even a "must" when it comes to reproduction now, as sperm is being harvested and frozen in droves. And with a healthy range of vibrators and sex toys on the market, we pretty much have it all covered. So if we do choose to be with a man, it should be one who adds value to our life. Most of us (hopefully) no longer view men as something to make us "complete," especially if we have good friends around us.

✎ **NOTE:** Gone are the days when women viewed marriage as a barometer to determine who they were in life. I would say the opposite is true now.

Ultimately, because our standards are much higher than ever before, when it comes to marriage, women have become over-qualified and men under-qualified. That's the reason we end up remaining single.

So you could say—based on all this information—that realistically, unless a woman gets married in her early to mid-twenties, when she is still young enough not to have seen much of the world, and therefore able to be manipulated and molded into family "wife life," the odds are pretty slim that she will ever marry at all.

✎ **NOTE:** I doubt that as many women under twenty-five have had affairs as older women, because they are so young in their outlook and are therefore happier with less (e.g., someone in their own age bracket and lifestyle parameter, such as the head cashier at Wal-Mart or manager of Starbucks).

When I was in my twenties, I would not have been in any way mature enough for an affair, nor would I have been interested in, or prepared for, the mental gymnastics required. I was too busy "being in my twenties," dating guys my age, contemplating making a life with someone. However, somehow here I am as an SUW writing a book about the art of having an affair.

✎ **NOTE TO SELF:** It's ironically funny the cards that life deals out to you sometimes!

The longer we wait to settle down, the more worldly and successful many of us SUWs become, and we know *exactly* how men feel about that. It makes it hard for us to suffer fools gladly—if at all—resulting in older, successful single women being the most messed up and left out demographic of them all, just *that much* too old and set in our ways to conform to being regular marriage material, but *that much* too young to be classed as spinsters.

The dating and mating universe seems to widen for men as they age (married or not) but narrows for women. Men seem to grow older and more "distinguished" (especially if they're wealthy), whereas women just seem to grow older!

There are definitely more women available to men as they get older and more successful, but fewer available men for women of the same standing.

✎ **NOTE TO SUWs:** Don't trade down and settle for less than you deserve in a partner just to fit into society. Even though sometimes we feel that if we dare to aim too high, we know we'll be destined to end up with slim pickings. (Tough! Keep aiming high, sisters!)

Apparently *Newsweek* has since admitted that their odds were way too pessimistic, although with the average age of a first marriage being twenty-five for women and twenty-seven for men, it is higher than ever before.

And so we arrive at the subject of this chapter: why women choose to take the next step and date an unavailable man (in this case, a married man). It is an interesting subject with many angles but no real definitive answer. My personal slant is that what you can't have is often more exciting and tantalizing than what you can. The ungettable is so much more interesting to the well-weathered, despondent SUW, and the challenge of it all is good exercise if she is getting tired of the gym.

We know we can settle for a regular Joe of a husband if we want one, but many of us don't want one. The longer we're single, the more we like it and the more selfish we become with our time.

🕐 **TIME MANAGEMENT SOLUTION NOTE:** Enter here the perfect setting for an affair with a married man.

If you can't find Mr. Right, an affair can be a very good substitute or solution, especially since you know you can remain on the lookout for your elusive life companion in tandem with seeing your MM. Your MM is not exclusive to you, so you needn't be to him either. On top of that, an affair carried out properly can give you a lot of what you do want—affection and good times—and little of what you don't want—commitment and hard work.

✎ **FACTUAL NOTE:** There is a high probability that an SUW who chooses to have affairs on a regular basis is suffering from commitment phobia brought on by enjoying her single, self-centered lifestyle too much.

Based on the fact that most of the single available men are either gay, "confused," or carrying so much baggage from previous relationships that they need a U-Haul truck and storage area for it, it's no surprise that so many SUWs embark upon affairs with a married man as a very viable option.

✎ **NOTE OF CONVENIENCE:** The beauty of an MM is that he is around when it's convenient to the SUW and not around when it's inconvenient for her. Perfect, no?

As an SUW, you will have tried everything in pursuit of a boyfriend. You will have done the bar and club scene, but that gets boring. You've also probably tried Match.com and other online methods as a way to meet other singles.

✎ **NOTE:** I tried the online route—just for research purposes, of course, not because I was in any way desperate...*honest!* And I found it hilariously funny and quite addictive in the beginning. But it became hugely depressing after a while. Looking into the faces of the "matches" out there and the e-mails I had to wade through from truly the least compatible selection of men on earth, I decided to resign from it shortly afterward.

I saw a new online dating service advertised recently that boasted "1,000 new singles" every hour! That's 24,000 a day! Has the world gone mad? Or has the whole world gone single—and is enjoying it?

As a further part of your quest as an SUW to find a mate, you may have joined the local gym, which you can't really afford, in hopes of finding "Mr. Right." But you didn't find him—just a load of beefcakes and gay men in tight shorts. So when Mr. Wrong-and-I'm-Married comes along, who happens to be very articulate, successful, attractive (unhappy and needy), and showing a great deal of interest in you, naturally you tend to be reeled in. You tell yourself it's wrong, but you'll worry about that later because, after all, he's the one who came on to you, right? Sounding familiar at all, ladies?

✎ **NOTE:** While being an annoying cliché, the saying "You can't help who you fall for" is often very true. You can be so attracted to a man and so smitten with him that even if he is married (but game for an affair), you will be compelled to go ahead with it. For all those who pour scorn on SUWs for embarking upon a tryst, I want you to know that we really tried the regular route; we really tried all the normal ways to meet and date eligible men. Those ways just didn't work!

If you're an SUW who plans to have kids (when you meet the right man), beware of having a *lengthy* affair because the problem here is that the carefree SUW you used to be—on the lookout for "eligibles" to mold a life with—suddenly becomes a mistress involved with a man who has already sculpted his own life and had his own kids.

Thus the ex-carefree SUW is now mired in the quicksand of a love triangle, throwing her energies into her MM, trying to get him to change by leaving his wife and kids, then dealing with the turmoil when he doesn't! This will leave you not only bitter and twisted—and wary of meeting any potentially single and good men—but often leaves your biological clock unable to function even if you did meet that guy you want to settle down and have kids with.

✎ **NOTE OF THEFT:** In this case, your MM has quite literally stolen your child-rearing years for his own pleasure and sexual gratification.

In a situation where the affair has dissolved, all you're left with are the memories (and hopefully a few gifts!), whilst the MM gets to go back, often virtually unscathed, to his unknowing (or uncaring) wife and children—perhaps even grandchildren too. You get to go back to an empty home, a quiet telephone, and a few frozen meals for one!

✎ **NOTE:** Perhaps some of the women who married in their twenties and who were therefore not eligible to be part of the *Newsweek* SUW survey are now the same boring, chunky housewives in their forties and fifties who are being cheated on by their husbands—husbands who'd rather be enjoying the company of those single thirty- and forty-something women *Newsweek* so vividly described. Basically it's all a game, a never-ending, vicious circle of adultery. But I know which woman I'd prefer to be—and it's definitely not the wife!

For a single woman involved with a married man, her affair, by definition, should be fun and romantic—and in the beginning it nearly always is.

✎ **A SASSY DEFINITION NOTE:** An affair is a relationship without the rules!

Your senses are on fire. You can't wait to see that person, especially when he tells you he is longing to be with you, not his wife, and that he is "counting the days until he sees you." It can all become quite intoxicating if you start to believe him, and you can end up almost feeling sorry for him having to *suffer* being with his wife as you gradually feel more and more needed by him. You may feel as if you're performing a service for the community.

✎ **NOTE TO MISTRESSES:** YOU NEED TO LET THAT ONE GO, PRONTO! Especially if you end up calling his wife in the future (as often happens) and you find out that he wasn't *suffering* at all! How stupid will you feel?

The beginning of an affair should be all about you, as ultimately you are the one agreeing to see him on his terms—accepting the fact that he is married. Make sure he knows that from the beginning!

You should embrace any and every opportunity to live the high life with him, and through him, enjoying the gifts, sex, passion, and travel that may—and in fact *should*—come your way!

✎ **NOTE TO MISTRESSES:** An affair with an older, wealthy MM is a great way to broaden your outlook. It can provide you excellent opportunities to do and see things in life that you might not normally get the chance to do (especially with a guy your own age), and if you pick the right MM, you can travel extensively, experience different cultures, and learn so much about the world in general.

You should *not* get involved in any domestic duties for him, such as sock washing, food shopping, or the boring duties that go with matrimony. Let the wife have those sorts of obligations.

Let his wife have the pleasure of washing his dirty laundry after he's been having fun with you. It's not your responsibility. And let them keep their money worries between themselves, and their conversations about how "little Jack is not doing well at school these days" should be had on *their* time. You should live your life as free as a bird—when you are with or without him!

There is, of course, the very real emotional downside to an affair, no matter how strong we try to be in the beginning, and which comes back to what you expect from your MM and how serious your relationship is. The woman desperately in love with her MM, the one who is begging him to leave his wife, is obviously going to be more emotionally vulnerable than the party girl who's just treating her MM as a sugar daddy stop-gap.

If you are in love with your MM (more on that later!), your feelings and innate nurturing instincts toward him may cause you to want to make a home for him. You may want to turn him into that Mr. Right you were originally seeking out before he came on to you and turned your world and your criteria upside down. In this case, the fact that the person you love (or think you love) is with someone else will naturally be very hard for you to deal with and is where the "some level of pain becoming your daily norm" reference I made earlier comes into play.

So, notwithstanding all the reasons one should or shouldn't have an affair, and to prevent any opportunity for doubt, the answer to why SUWs do so is because of the severe shortage of available, single, normal men out there. Offset that against the obvious abundance of unhappily married men and players looking for an extramarital relationship, or at least a bit on the side, and the question is answered.

✎ **NOTE:** With such an equation, is it really any wonder, or even scandalous, why so many single women actually do date married men? Definitely putting the *sin* into single as they do so!

Whatever your reasons for your affair, I urge you, please don't let it just be love. Don't treat your MM as a regular boyfriend. Don't hang on his every word, and *never* discount the fact that he can't make any real plans with you. And try not to beat yourself up whilst he is with his wife and not you, or you will become black and blue on the inside.

If you do care about the guy, you will at some point start comparing yourself to his wife. It's only natural, and it's actually quite intriguing. You'll have questions like, "Why is he with me?" "What is his wife lacking?" "What is she like?" "What does she look like?" But one burning question will always eat away at you: "Why won't he leave her for me?" Especially if you are all those wonderful things he keeps saying you are!

✎ **REALITY NOTE:** The answer is simple. It is because he loves her more than you. If it were anything other than that, he would change his situation in order to be with you. SUWs, you have to deal with that truth. Whatever line he tries to feed you, that is the bottom one.

The irony of all this is that many SUWs who resort to dating MMs are more often than not very attractive, successful, and outgoing women who would have no problem getting *anyone*. Friends, usually those who are already part of a couple, will ask you, "Why you are selling yourself short by being with a man who has another woman, knowing you will never be number one in his life?" (How bored I had gotten at hearing that, although its truth annoyed me so much at the same time!)

This chapter really has no beginning and no end—and no definitive answers. Your choices are purely based on your personal feelings and interactions with the other party. Anyone who enters into an affair with an MM will have her own reasons for doing so, which can range from loneliness, low self-esteem, pure infatuation, or a short-term fix, to believing she's found the love she's really looking for. For some, it may even be a way to better their lifestyle. And there is no shame in that. In fact, ironically, that is something you would have in common with your MM too.

All this book can really do is open your eyes to situations you may be in, or may become entangled in. It aims to give you another dimension on life from people who have been where you are. I hope it will make some things easier for you to handle throughout your affair, as well as give you the strength to make decisions with a broader perspective.

I hope too that it will make you think about the most important question: "Are you living the life you deserve with the person who deserves you, or are you compromising and giving up on your real dreams?"

If you believe you're having a relationship with your MM because you love him, be very careful. I can't emphasize that enough. It will end in tears: *yours!* Better to love him, but not to be "in love" with him, or you will be the one picking up the pieces when he eventually makes it clear that he isn't going to leave his wife for you—even if he does lead you to believe that he's planning to.

Finally, I also learned that the other very valid reason women choose to have an affair with an MM is because not every woman wants to get married, so having an affair can be just what she needs in her life. I asked some of the women I interviewed why they, as single women (their ages ranged between thirty and sixty-two), chose to have affairs. Here are some of their answers:

MISTRESS A: "A married man offers a stop-gap, a placeholder for me while I look for 'Mr. Right.' I used my MM as batting practice and thought that being loved and adored by a man would give me a happy and healthy glow that would attract other, better and more suitable men. I needed something going on in my life because there just aren't any eligible men out there…"

The MM in this story was found out by his wife and went on to dump Mistress A, saying he couldn't be with her as she was the reason why his wife—whom he professed never to have loved and didn't sleep with—had left him and turned his children against him.

She was in complete shock and couldn't understand it. How could he go from wanting to be with her every minute possible to not wanting to be with her at all, even when his circumstances ended up allowing it? What hurt her even more is that he went on a sabbatical to the

Far East, met a flight attendant on his trip and brought her home and married her shortly afterward!

The hardest thing for Mistress A was that she and the MM worked together, which was how they'd met. She had to continue to deal with him on a daily basis and shortly afterward his new wife *too*.

The result is that she's still going to therapy to try and get over the whole sorry story of her affair.

MISTRESS B: Likes the fact that MMs *are* so "unavailable." She is a single mother who, after two useless husbands, is done with marriage and needs, and enjoys, her space. She likes the financial benefits of seeing her current wealthy MM, and because he has so little time to give her and feels so guilty about it, he tries to make up for it with generous gifts and payment of bills. That suits her fine, as she is not in love with him, and the less time she has to spend with him, the better in her book!

Previously she was madly in love with an MM for six years and desperately wanted him to leave his wife. He had a high-profile position in the hotel world and never would. She dated other people, and he couldn't handle it. They ended the affair, but eventually he came back. Now it's on her terms, and she is no longer in love with him. But it's a familiar pairing, and it fills a gap in her world until something better comes along. She would die if he left his wife for her now, though. (Boy, how things change!)

MISTRESS C: Wasn't looking for an MM, but one pursued her. She eventually fell totally in love with him and with how wonderfully he treated her in the beginning—he was a lot older, very wealthy, and very generous. But she fell for the wrong man and foolishly believed in him. Although not actually married, he was in a ten-year relationship and had two small children. He turned out to be a compulsive liar and a serial philanderer on all accounts.

He professed to want to be with Mistress C so badly that he uprooted her from her life in the States to be close to him in Europe. He prevaricated and never made any effort whatsoever to make a change in his lifestyle, but continued lying to his mistress, feigning that he *wanted* to.

In the end, Mistress C was totally in love with the guy and at her wit's end as to why he wouldn't reveal their affair to this woman he wasn't even married to. She was so disheartened about it all that she called his common-law wife to reveal it to her in person.

Result? The common-law wife didn't throw him out. She pathetically let him stay and continued to let him walk all over her (no doubt buffered by his money—he was a multi-millionaire), and turned him against Mistress C. Go figure!

Mistress C had her revenge on them both, but that's another story. She finally got over the whole business and tried to reassemble her life back in the States.

✎ **A FINAL NOTE TO MISTRESSES:** Always remember that we as women have the choice whether to have the affair or not. There is always the option of running in the opposite direction when you find out he is married. It's interesting that we so often don't!

chapter 5

How to Recognize If a Man Is Married

Despite What He Tells You

 You'd think being married would be relatively hard to keep a secret. But never underestimate the capacity of a man to lie or at least to *withhold* the truth, especially a married man on a mission.

You can only *hope* that when you first encounter your MM, he will be upfront and honest with you—a complete oxymoron for any MM—about the fact that he's married. A lot of times they will tell you right away, quickly followed by how unhappy they are at home, but at least you know where you stand and where he "lies," so to speak. I believe that what you know about you can deal with. Knowledge is power and all that jazz.

If you have all the information at hand, you can make an educated decision as to whether you wish to move forward with him or not. If you are having the wool pulled over your eyes by a duplicitous, "sheepish" moron, that's not good for you at all.

✎ **NOTE TO NAIVE, UNAWARE SISTERS:** If he is married and not telling you, all he is foolishly doing by keeping it a secret is giving himself a short-term hiatus in which to enjoy sex and good times with you. These good times will pale into insignificance for him as soon as you find out the truth and go totally ballistic—and find out the truth, you will. Trust me.

So let's take a look at MMs who lie—the calculating ones who tell you they're not married in order to get you to sleep with them and see them again (sometimes just the first bit actually). The ones who try to reel you in so that by the time they do tell you their "situation," you will have fallen for them hook, line, and sinker (or rather stinker).

✎ **NOTE TO All SISTERS:** This particular group of MMs is commonly known as BASTARDS!

Now, if there aren't any visible "wedding signals" on the man in question and if he happens to be exuding an "I'm a single guy on the lookout" kind of breezy attitude, then asking him if he's married probably won't be the first question on your lips. Why would it be?

✎ **NOTE TO SISTERS (and PLEASE remember this one):** Trust no man until he proves himself, and even then be wary. I would strongly advise you to do your research early and use your head, not just your heart. Read on to see what I mean.

So, sisters, let's say you are out and about one evening, mingling and enjoying yourself, and you meet a guy you like. You're thrilled and relieved to see that he isn't wearing a wedding ring, but do not assume anything! Absence of a ring does not mean he *isn't* married, or at least not one-half of a couple. It could just mean that he chooses not to wear a wedding ring (some men don't do bling).

If he is married and doesn't wear the appropriate piece of "commitment jewelry," then he's already making a statement. And therefore he is not going to offer the information on a platter that he's married. If you don't ask, he won't tell. *(Not before he gets you into bed, anyway.)* Men's "version" of the truth remember, and "withholding of the truth" is not classed as lying.

☞ **HARSH ADVICE NOTE TO SISTERS:** ASK! ASK! ASK!

If he is married (and further down the line when you do find out about his true marital status), his weak alpha male response might be, "Well, you didn't *ask* me if I was married." Or even better, "Well, yes, technically I am married, but it's only on paper. It's not marriage in the true sense of the word; I'm not happy. I don't love her. We don't sleep together anymore." (As if *that* statement makes it okay to cheat on his other half!) But my favorite is, "If we didn't have children, I wouldn't still be with her. But I was scared that if I told you the truth, you wouldn't be interested in me." (INSERT LARGE YAWN HERE.)

✎ **NOTE:** I'm sure you'll agree with me that such feeble excuses don't even warrant our discussion.

Now, here's a true story for you. I knew a guy (let's call him "Antonio the Italian" for the sake of this story) who did exactly the aforementioned to his mistress (let's call her Jenny), and she couldn't believe that she didn't see it coming.

Antonio worked as the right-hand man to an extremely well-known, international unmarried playboy, whom Jenny was casually dating.

Antonio and Jenny met through his playboy boss when he was enlisted to look after her and chauffeur her around as required. She found his company far more refreshing and edgy than his aging boss (and, yes, he was drop-dead gorgeous, possessing the swarthy looks that a mixture of Mediterranean blood provides). And even though she was literally trading down to this younger guy on a modest salary, they had so much chemistry going on that she decided to take a chance and respond to the very obvious advances he was making to her.

He was so "Italiano" and had such a carefree attitude about life that Jenny said, "Marriage was not something I would have ever, ever associated with him."

To make a long story short, after many wonderful liaisons, they fell in love, lust, obsession—call it what you will. They had it all going on. It was mutual and it was wonderful. So wonderful, Jenny said, that when he called her one Thursday morning in late November, well over a month into their relationship, and said there was something he needed to tell her, something he couldn't tell her on the phone, she had no idea what he was talking about.

She insisted that he tell her whatever it was then and there, as he lived over an hour away and there was no way she could wait that long. She thought he was breaking up with her (not something Jenny was typically familiar with).

She asked him if he was gay, and he said no. She asked him if he was sick or in trouble, and he said no. She asked him if he was seeing someone else and when he said, "No, but keep going," she knew. Only then did the possibility of him being married enter her head, and only then did the question stutter from her lips. There was nothing else left it could be.

They had always needed to be fairly secretive due to the delicate situation they were in. Although Jenny was no longer seeing Antonio's boss, it wouldn't look good for either of them if he found out they were an item. This meant that Antonio mostly came over to her place, or they went out in the city rather than risk being seen in the small countryside village where he lived on his boss's estate. Thinking back, Jenny realized that this was *exactly* how he had managed to cover up his marital status for so long. He had been clever enough not to show any obvious signs whatsoever, although as Jenny later conceded: "Love is blind!"

Jenny said she felt totally and utterly blown away, especially when she heard the rest. She wouldn't give me the details of why Antonio professed he "had" to stay with his wife. But it was mainly due to the wife finding out that he'd slept with the boss's supermodel girlfriend a year previously—a little over and above what his bodyguard and chauffeuring duties had called for, no doubt! His wife knew, and she was blackmailing him over it, threatening to tell *their* boss if he tried to leave her (more on that in a minute).

✎ **NOTE TO SELF:** If he *was* lying, it was certainly quite an original story, to say the least.

So poor Jenny was actually hit with two disturbing pieces of information to digest that morning—all before 9:30 a.m., and before any coffee had passed her lips. Not only had her gorgeous, handsome lover suddenly turned into a lying, cheating, married bastard who had conned her for more than a month, but he had also slept with one of the biggest supermodels on the planet. Jenny didn't know which was worse. She didn't know whether to feel pissed off that he was a serial liar and adulterer, or insecure about her petite frame, thinking, "Why would he be with me when he could get a world-famous model?"

Oh, and I referred to the high-profile guy as being *their* boss, because as it turned out, Antonio's lovely wife worked alongside her husband for the same guy. When he told Jenny who his wife was, she realized she had met her on many occasions at their boss's estate (when visiting on dinner dates with their "Lord and Master"). Ironically, Jenny said, the thing that stuck in her throat the most was the fact that Antonio's wife was blond and Antonio had always made jokes about blondes. (Funny how in the big picture it's often the little things that bug you most, isn't it?)

Anyway, at the end of the day, it turned out his wife was the household chef. She'd often cooked for Jenny on her dinner dates and visits. Jenny told me that she thanked her lucky stars the chef hadn't been aware of the truth, as she might have poisoned her risotto! Another ironic truth hit Jenny too: the wife could cook and Jenny couldn't— the trauma and insecurity seemed never-ending!

In a nutshell, it was a real mess, but amazingly Jenny didn't walk away. "Italiano Antonio" apparently fed her such a good story that she said if she was being honest, she probably actually wanted him more— especially with the validation in her mind that he could have supermodels but chose to be with her. *Pathetic*, as she later agreed.

What happened further down the line was no picnic, and it got pretty messy. Jenny said she suffered a great deal emotionally through it all. In the end, everyone found out about everything, making this a perfect example of the damage and destruction that can be caused by a duplicitous MM trying to have his cake and eat it too (probably baked by his wife in this case!). Jenny said she often reflects and wonders where they all are now...but never for long.

Okay, so back to the telltale signs of whether a man is married or not and how you can outsmart him in order to find out. Naturally, sporting a wedding ring is the biggest and easiest giveaway.

✎ **NOTE:** A ring is no guarantee, though, because even if he does normally wear it 24/7, he still could have slipped it off if he is on a mission to meet someone else—if he is on a mission to meet you.

Sisters, I urge you to do as much due diligence (otherwise known as DD) as you can when you meet a man these days, especially one you like. Look for an indentation where a ring could have been lodged on his left hand shortly before he started talking to you, or perhaps a tan line from a recent family holiday to Disney World, as the sun may have left a white mark where a ring normally resides.

Next on the list of "MM red flag alerts" is the fact that a married man will never give you his home phone number. This one, however, can't be used as a fair benchmark because it isn't a must when it comes to communication these days. If his home number did happen to be his only means of contact, and he gave it to you, it would definitely mean he was unmarried. (It could also mean he doesn't own a mobile phone, which would mean he's behind the times, too tight, or too poor to have one—maybe all three and hence the reason why he's single.)

So this can't be used as a concrete clue since most men you meet wouldn't be giving their home phone number out in this tech-savvy age we live in. Of the men you meet, 99.9 percent of them will be easily contactable via portable devices. He will undoubtedly give you his mobile number for starters.

He may have two mobiles—*look out for that.* If he does have two but he won't give you both numbers, question it. If he's married, one number will be his private mobile number, which his wife knows nothing about, and he will only give you that one. If he's single, though, he'll give you both or will at least explain why he has two phones!

✎ **NOTE TO SUSPICIOUS SISTERS:** Even though you might not want both mobile phone numbers, just take them as a test, and call them (blocking your number, of course) to check that it is his voice on both of the recorded messages and that his voicemail content ties in with what he has told you about himself.

He will probably give you his work number next.

✎ **NOTE TO SISTERS WHO ARE DOING THEIR "DD":** See whether he gives you any instructions when it comes to calling him at the office, such as who you should say you are, how you should deal with his P.A., and so on. A married man will be more inclined to do this than a single one.

Last but not least will be his e-mail address.

🖱 **NOTE TO CYBER-SISTERS:** See if he gives you a work e-mail and/or a private one. See which one he says you should use most. His job and/or position will determine how communicative he can be on his company e-mail address. If he uses a personal Hotmail address or something similar, monitor the times of any e-mails he sends you in the evening, because a lot of MMs use the computer at home to e-mail their mistress before and after the wife goes to bed. The wife, who will just be glad he's home for a change, will assume he is working on an important project. *(She wouldn't be far wrong, either!)*

As you can see, with these strong communication channels—and that's not even touching on SMS messaging, BlackBerrys, Treos, and wireless laptops—it wouldn't be until a few dates down the line that you'd be hankering after a home number anyway.

🗝 **TIP FOR SISTERS:** Don't give him *your* home phone number. You can't retract it if you made a wrong choice of guy.

After a few dates, you'll likely expect to have visited his abode or at least be invited. If he's married, and has fooled you for that long, he won't have a place to take you. That should set off some warning bells in itself, even before the phone number issue rears its head. Some wealthy MMs have their own secret apartments. I will let you do the DD on that one if you ever go there. But look in the cupboards for everyday items, and look at the photos on the walls. Everyone has photos in their home, so if there are none, it may smack of being a rented sex pad. MMs without money and resources may borrow a friend's place in an attempt to fool you. Again, do the DD and be aware.

✎ **NOTE TO SISTERS WHO ARE BEING TAKEN FOR A RIDE:** Watch to see if he switches off his mobile when he's with you or puts it on silent. If he does take calls, watch his face when he answers. If it's a call from an inquisitive wife *(a rare combination)*, he will be put on the spot to have to talk to her in front of you. See if he squirms and lies in front of your very eyes, or whether he steps out of the room to do it in private.

These pointers are not guarantees, of course, just helpful tips. But I do hope you are getting my point about being aware and questioning certain things that you previously may have taken for granted—*do your DD!*

✎ **NOTE TO REMEMBER:** Don't take him at face value, sisters, as he could have many faces!

If all of this information is not enough to ensure that you determine whether your new man is lying to you (and, my God, you must be dumb if it isn't), pay attention to when and how he calls you. An MM, unless he is away on company business, will rarely be able to call you late at night and hold the usual intimate conversations that you both effortlessly enjoy throughout the day—for obvious reasons (often two to three hundred chunky pounds of obvious reasons!).

So watch to see if your contact with him mysteriously dwindles off in the evening, when he might be home with the wife and kids. His phone may be switched off during this time, or when he sees your number, he may have to let your call go to voicemail. If so, he will call you first thing the next morning to get his excuses in early.

If you are still having niggling doubts about his marital status, examine any late-night calls he does happen to make to you, or leave him an "urgent" message (about something trivial) on his voicemail to see if he gets back to you in a timely manner. If he's married and is calling you from the marital home, it will be a quick call—very quick. He may step out into the garden to use his phone, taking the trash out for his wife at the same time. The family dog, the one he told you he doesn't have, might be barking in the background. And if he is still lying to you then, he will give you an excuse as to why the call has to be such a short one.

Listen for excuses such as a low battery on his mobile, being tired and needing to get a good night's sleep, having an early start the next day, needing to get off the line in order to make his weekly conference call to the States, not feeling well, and so on.

✎ **NOTE:** Store all this information in your subconscious, sisters. You may need to revert back to it one day.

If you think I'm talking rubbish, you are in denial. Please take care to safeguard yourself from getting hurt. Please do your investigations and your DD at the beginning. And, hey, here's the upside. If you were wrong about him being married, and are confident about him being single (and a great catch), then fantastic! That will be a bonus, and your work is already done.

RECAP NOTES FOR ALL POTENTIALLY UNAWARE MISTRESSES:

- Check for a wedding ring mark/indentation on his left finger.
- Ask to visit his home if you are in any doubt about his marital status. Don't take no for an answer on this one; push it until he has to deal with your request.
- As you get to know him, see whether he takes and makes "private" phone calls in front of you or whether he finds the need to step out and make them.
- Note the times of his calls to you outside of office hours, and see if you find him unobtainable late at night.
- Note whether you send him text messages that he doesn't reply to for hours or whether, in fact, he asks you not to send him text messages at all during certain periods.
- Make sure you get his business card when you first meet him, and go home and Google him. See if you can find out more

about him before you next speak or take his call. (The better "catch" you suspect he is, the more you should do this.)

- If you meet him whilst he is with a group of friends, listen to their conversation and observe their interaction with each other. That alone should give you some clues as to whether he is married or single.

- My last point on this subject is that if he does have a wedding ring on and has opened up to you, telling you the truth about being married (although he may tell you he is in the midst of separating, of course), at least note how he refers to his wife in the conversation and what sort of demeanor he has when describing her and his situation. Nobody wants a true bastard or complete serial adulterer, so look to see if there is an ounce of humility and contriteness in his explanation as to why he is about to cheat on his wife...*with you.*

✎ **FINAL NOTE:** Remember that the first thing an adulterous married man will always tell you is that he "doesn't normally do this kind of thing."

✎ **NOTE TO SELF:** Yeah, right! And I'm the Queen of England!

Good luck out there, sisters. It's a real minefield, so be sure to keep the DD faith going strong.

chapter 6

"My Wife Doesn't Understand Me"

And Other "Get Out" Clichés

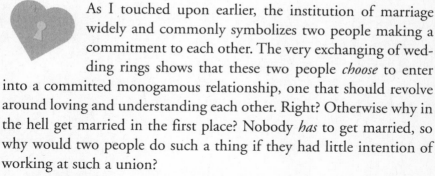 As I touched upon earlier, the institution of marriage widely and commonly symbolizes two people making a commitment to each other. The very exchanging of wedding rings shows that these two people *choose* to enter into a committed monogamous relationship, one that should revolve around loving and understanding each other. Right? Otherwise why in the hell get married in the first place? Nobody *has* to get married, so why would two people do such a thing if they had little intention of working at such a union?

This leads nicely into one of the oldest and most clichéd lines in the MM's handbook of quotes: "My wife doesn't understand me."

Now, "My wife doesn't understand me" may not be the first line in your MM's repertoire, but it will certainly feature in conversation soon after he meets you, mainly because he will definitely want you to know (and believe) that he "doesn't do *this sort of thing* often." (He may even start believing it himself!)

✎ **NOTE:** Remember to refer to my advice in chapter five on "How to Recognize If a Man Is Married," if you find yourself in this situation, just in case he is trying to pull a fast one on you.

One can't help but wonder if it's the wives who don't understand them, or if it's men who don't want to be understood (or simply don't make the effort).

How about this for an analogy? Maybe it's *because* the wife totally and utterly understands her husband that they have problems to begin with. (Remember, the characteristics of the married man *you* see and have feelings for will not be the same ones she sees at home.) So, the fact that his wife *does* understand him and knows exactly what makes him tick could be the very reason (in her eyes) why she chooses to push him away, only tolerating him when she has to (for the sake of the children, of course).

The result is that whatever got them to that point, from the day they originally said "I do," has led the wife to cease putting in the effort required to make her husband happy and build their marriage. Which results in him going elsewhere to make himself happy! And as he travels on this destructive monorail to happiness, he will mentally place any blame, for his straying, on his wife (whom he supposedly married for better or worse). Because she "didn't understand him," he was left with no option but to go out and cheat on her. He will see this as absolution for any wrongdoing. Furthermore, any couples therapy or marriage counseling they may end up going to will revolve around *her* not meeting *his* needs.

Beyond the wife who simply gives up, there will always be the "mousy" wives, which I refer to as "mousewives."

Mousewives, whether they have the capacity to "understand" their husbands or not, don't stand a chance in hell of him ever being faithful, as these wives are never enough for their man and never will be, especially if they married young and their lives have taken different paths: hers to domesticity and suburbia and his to "the world." (See chapter three, "How and Why Married Men Stray.")

Mousewives like these, who act as doormats, don't present their husband with any challenges. They typically have a low sex drive (and low expectations of life in general), and the only sexual position they usually allow, or even know about, is missionary.

✎ **NOTE:** Most men love to be challenged by strong women; it turns them on.

The benefit of the mousewife, though, is that she doesn't usually possess the imagination required to ever suspect her husband is having an affair. Consequently, for any MM who wants to cheat, this is the best type of wife to have. She'll believe anything he tells her, so he'll be able to get away with murder. *(Just make sure it's not yours!)*

The MM who has a "dormant doormat of a mousewife" at home might describe her as follows: "I have a great wife; she doesn't have a bad bone in her body. She is loyal and has done nothing wrong, and she is a *wonderful* mother to my children. Our sex life has become almost nonexistent, but I couldn't leave her; it would hurt her too much. She relies on me emotionally; she'd never survive, and she does-n't have very many friends."

✎ **NOTE TO MISTRESSES:** You'd think if the wife was that great, she'd at least give him a hand job occasionally, eh girls?

So whichever angle of an MM being misunderstood we are sup-posed to believe, we should at least agree that if a married man is play-ing around whilst in a supposedly exclusive relationship, it is because his needs are not being met to his satisfaction by the person he's with. (His boxes are not being checked, for want of a better expression).

People only look for sex outside a relationship if they aren't happy—period. However, there is the odd exception to this rule with the few MMs who can't keep their zipper closed, the ones who will play around no matter how good their relationship is. (They are dan-gerous to all concerned, including themselves).

✎ **NOTE TO SISTERS:** We've all bumped into the cads of married men—the type who prop up the bar and buy you and your friends drinks all night, whilst professing to have such a wonderful marriage and loving wife—who, when the bar closes, make advances on you, expecting you to "carry on the party" after-hours!

But for the most part, when one half of a relationship cheats, it's due to him or her not being satisfied and therefore looking elsewhere for someone who can meet and take care of his or her emotional and physical needs.

✎ **NOTE:** Again, one wonders if wives are at fault for not meeting their husbands' needs? Or are husbands' needs beyond reasonably meetable?

Your MM may also use the line, "There just isn't any chemistry between me and my wife anymore," which is basically the same as "my wife doesn't understand me"—just packaged a little differently, in an attempt to throw you off the scent for a while.

✎ **NOTE TO MISTRESSES:** Wouldn't you just love to question that statement? I mean, there was chemistry between them at some point; there must have been in order to get married and have kids. So where did it go? Who gave up? And more to the point, why on earth stay?

When I interviewed one particularly indignant fifty-eight-year-old MM on this subject, he replied: "I didn't say my wife *doesn't* understand me; I said there was no chemistry between us anymore, no passion," as though he really believed there was a huge difference between the two statements. (And for the record, in case this man is reading, you did originally say, "My wife doesn't understand me." But that's okay. After all, they're only words, and you *are* getting on a bit!)

✎ **NOTE OF OBSERVATION:** If it's true that chemistry does indeed disappear within marriage, there must be millions of "chemically imbalanced" people walking around out there.

This particular MM continued describing his situation to me: "We've been together so long that things are more routine between us now, not like when I am with my mistress, where everything is new and exciting." Basically, here he was saying that he was addicted to the sex with his mistress and how she makes him feel, and that he could sustain his home life in the meantime because it wasn't *that bad*.

✎ **NOTE:** The mistress filled his void (just as he was undoubtedly filling hers—HA! (Laugh out loud!)

✎ **INQUISITIVE NOTE:** Does an MM get tempted to experiment the newly practiced sexual positions he enjoys with his mistress with his wife too? I doubt it, as that would be a red flag for her, but on the other hand, how could he revert back to being satisfied with missionary ever again?

The premise of this chapter is to let you know that your MM isn't happy at home because he isn't being loved in the way he wants to be (and we know men think, *and love*, purely with their dicks)—meaning he isn't being taken care of in the bedroom in the way he wants to be.

It never ceases to amaze me how many couples stop having sex at some point in their marriage. I have interviewed men who haven't had sex with their partners in the range of two to eight years, yet bizarrely professed that "everything else" between them was good. They also stated weakly that "you can't have it all!"

✎ **NOTE:** Why not? Of course you can have it all. It just takes that four-letter word to make it happen: W-O-R-K!

✎ **SIDE NOTE OF HUMOR:** What food is the most known to put women off sex?

ANSWER: *Wedding cake!*

Some of the married men I interviewed went on to qualify their situations with the now-so-predictable comment: "But she's such a wonderful mother to my children and has done a brilliant job of raising them. That's all that matters to me!"

✎ **NOTE TO THOSE WHO HAVE HEARD IT ALL BEFORE:** Oh, pass me the bucket, *puh-leeze!* Do these guys only want a nanny, or do they want the wife and the healthy relationship they *thought* they'd signed up for all those years ago when they said "I do" (and "Good-bye bank account")?

By the way, I've never heard anyone say, "She's such a bad mother." Have you? Of course not! All mothers love their children and are good mothers on the whole. So again, this is just another get-out clause from him (another *guilt* line).

If an MM had the balls to put in writing what he really thought of his marriage and his wife, I think it could give everyone involved some clarity. It might read something like this...

✒ **NOTE FROM CHEATER:** "Look, my wife takes care of my children, which suits me because I couldn't do it on my own. I have my own busy important life. I have to work and travel. But I do love the kids and I do always call to say goodnight when I'm away. They are housed, well clothed and cared for, taken to and from school and anywhere else they need to go by her (I could never do all that, thank you very much. I have golf to fit in!).

"My wife is good at it (and she really enjoys it all), and by devoting her life to the home and kids, she allows me the opportunity to live my life to its fullest. She's so busy with her housework and stuff that she's usually too tired to ask very much of me (or about me—thank God!). When I come home to the family unit, my meal is ready (I can't cook, and I'd hate to have to live off those TV dinners or meal-for-one-things).

"In addition, my closet is full of clean shirts and laundry (I can't iron, nor do I want to). So yes, I have to say that my wife is hugely important to me. She is everything: she's my cook, my nanny, and my domestic help all in one. I need her in my life.

"Oh, and okay, well, we don't have any chemistry and I don't have sex with her unless I *have to* (or sometimes if I'm really horny or drunk—or both), but that side of things doesn't bother me because I have my mistress for that, whom I see as often as possible. And her? Wow! Now there's a woman who really is something else..."

As you can see, for the married man, it's easier to take a lover and lie his pants off (quite literally), than try to work on the existing problems he and his wife have. And that, dear mistresses, is the real reason he is with you in the first place.

✎ **RECAP NOTE:** It's easier for him to deflect his issues by taking on a mistress than to have to deal with them!

A quote from one MM, who hasn't had sex with his wife in eight years (and doesn't want to): "I don't know how she thinks I manage," he said, "because she knows what a sexual person I am." He also told me that he tries to get to bed way after she does to ensure she's asleep by the time he hits the sack. What a sad way to live!

✎ **NOTE:** Sorry to be repetitive, but cheaters are cowards when all is said and done. There is no getting around that fact! Just reminding you again in case you lapsed in your train of thought since chapter three.

Now, the catch in all of this is that most of the grievances between the MM and his wife may stem from the fact that he spends far too much time away from her and the family home, allowing him less time to *try* to be understood, and less and less time (not) to address their existing problems. He is likely putting his time to more pleasant and advantageous use, such as the company of other women, thus creating more problems in the long run. (But as we know, cheating MMs mainly think in terms of the short run).

In a deteriorating marriage, the MM won't be overly concerned that his wife is unhappy too and that he should be making more of an effort to understand *her*. He will, however, be extremely pleased that she can't resort as easily to having an affair as her method of escape. Even if she wanted one, it would be too difficult to manage—especially if she is busy being a mousewife and a mother to young children—juggling babysitting and chef obligations in order to facilitate the smooth running of her husband's lifestyle, usually blissfully unaware that he is playing the field at the same time.

After completing her daily full-time job of looking after her husband and kids, she's too whacked to have energy left over for extramarital affairs. (Hell, she can hardly sleep with her own husband, let alone anybody else's!)

✎ **SUGGESTION NOTE TO WIVES:** If you're smart, you'll *try* to make the necessary time to sleep with somebody else's husband; it beats taking up needlework to relieve the boredom and frustration. If you're a stay-at-home wife, you might want to look at options such as the postman, gardener, or plumber—basically anyone who can service *you* as an extra service to the one he was coming to the house to carry out anyway. You'll probably wonder what took you so long. And after all, your husband is doing it—so why shouldn't you?

Another much younger MM I interviewed, who was on the brink of having an affair, told me that after nine years of marriage he did in fact still fancy his wife, and he did love her. He said it in a way that seemed to surprise him (and me too, considering he was flirting outrageously with me). But he complained that she didn't love him in the way he loved her (whatever way that was). He said that since the kids had been born (ages seven and nine), everything had changed. He felt she didn't make time for him anymore, and whined that she no longer made him feel special.

✎ **NOTE:** This guy is worth millions. They have a live-in *au pair* and a driver and every type of assistant—and assistance—the wife could possibly need. So what valid reason could she honestly find for not having time for him? Indifference, that's what!

These examples make me the most perplexed, amazed as to why the husband doesn't see what's going on and accept that they have a bad marriage and deal with it, rather than putting his energies into contemplating an affair, coupled with rolling home drunk at 4 a.m. as a way of masking his unhappiness. This particular MM is a hugely intelligent guy who commands a team of people within his own company and makes split-second decisions every day, yet he can't deal with an issue that's dictating his life and suffocating his personal happiness.

✎ **NOTE OF COMPARISON—MMs TO WELL-KNOWN PEOPLE:** This is a typical case where an MM has huge balls in the workplace but is pussy-whipped by his wife in the home (in other words, he is Bill Gates in the boardroom but SpongeBob in the bedroom).

So the wife has everything she could ever want financially and materially, but deep down there is no love between them. She blames it on being "too busy with the kids," while he uses being "too busy making money" as his excuse (even though earning the money involves having fun traveling the world, entertaining clients at all the best places, and sleeping with other women, but hey, just more of those silly, unimportant details!).

I guess for wives in this situation, it's all about the money in the end. It's no wonder the MM looks outside for the emotion and affection he craves. So often in cases like these, it's only the arguments that he and his wife have left in common, and their disparity becomes the only thing keeping them together. (Remember what I said about misery loving company? It's so true.)

This story is a good example of complacency and indifference in a young married couple, a situation of two double negatives, where the root of the problem never actually gets addressed. As this pair grows unhappily old together, they can proudly look back on their many affairs and how they "stayed together because of the kids," who were probably dying to escape the tense atmosphere they were brought up in.

✎ **NOTE:** What a lame chestnut of an excuse "having kids" has become for a couple to stay together. If they'd acted with more responsibility and hadn't had them in the first place, they wouldn't be in this situation. No relationship is worth tolerating other people's crap for, kids or no kids!

I heard later that the MM in question ended up dabbling in an affair (still rolling home drunk at 4 a.m., apparently), which enabled his wife, after one drunken occasion too many, to access his mobile phone and find text messages and e-mails from the woman he was "interacting" with. The result? The wife made a scene, packed her bags, and left. The MM told the "other woman" never to contact him again (as though it was *her fault* for responding to his intense advances in the first place). Men, huh?

I wonder if the wife ever came back (for more helpings of misery and denial) or if in fact she did them both a favor and cut loose. This man is extremely rich, so we already know the answer will be that she came back because she missed him so much (i.e., his money). No doubt his little escapades cost him dearly. Oh well, *c'est la vie*, as they say.

So from this type of couple living such an empty, separate existence—who want for nothing materially but are devoid of love and intimacy—let us consider the married couple who hardly have two pennies to rub together—yet they have so much love and respect for each other and they make things work come hell or high water. That's more of a tribute to the institute of marriage, don't you think?

$ FINANCIAL NOTE: Proving that money can't buy you love, but that it sure as hell can be used to screw a wayward husband very nicely, especially if the situation gets as far as divorce. This is why, sisters, I try to hit home the message: Don't date or marry *poor* men. Don't be a mistress to a poor MM; as you already know he'll end up hurting you by staying with his wife in the end. And, SUWs, don't marry a poor man, as you already know he'll end up hurting you by taking on a mistress in the end!

Whether a wife or a mistress, both will need to use money as leverage at some point in their relationships. They actually have more in common than one would think.

If the MM went to the trouble to treat his wife more like his mistress (great travel, wining and dining at all the best restaurants, and wonderful gifts), his wife might make more effort with him, and she just might "understand him." (Mistresses, by the way, if you're not getting any of these nice things, then you're doing it all wrong!)

But it's far easier for an MM to run the risk of getting caught, hurting people, and paying dearly financially, than *ever* to have the balls to tell his wife it's over.

As a mistress, always remember (even on good days) that you have chosen to be with a man who would rather conduct a duplicitous relationship with you than sit down with his wife or partner and tell her, "These are the reasons (A, B, C, D, E) that I can't be with you anymore, so what are we going to do about it?" Whatever happened to straight talking, eh?

✎ **NOTE TO MISTRESSES:** By allowing him to lose himself in a relationship with you, you are ultimately facilitating the MM so that he won't have to deal with things at home. That's okay, but be aware of it, that's all.

🗝 **BONUS TIP:** "Ultimatums" to your MM can come in quite handy if you want to kick things up a notch. Testing him is always a good thing to do.

Because we now know that the unhappy MM is weak and cowardly, we realize that he doesn't have the strength to upset the apple cart of life he has with his wife, nor does he have the strength to deal with the changes and ramifications if the cart topples. (Isn't it interesting to note that he is so fearful of change yet not fearful of cheating?)

Imagine all those joint friends he and his wife have together, all those boring couples they go out to dinner with on Saturday nights. Far too complicated for him to tell his wife it's over because of important factors like that. Consequently, there will be a place for mistresses in this world for a very long time to come!

✎ **NOTE TO MISTRESSES:** By the way, your MM won't be very bothered by what you're doing on Saturday nights. (And I hope it doesn't involve you sitting at home pining for him. That would be so futile.)

Basically, as long as the MM and his little world are turning smoothly, everything is just fine for all concerned. Not only are men fantastic liars, but most MMs are usually great actors as well (you may or may not see that side of him). And we can only *imagine* the award-winning performance he is putting on at home for his wife, who ultimately doesn't suspect him—or just doesn't care anymore.

An MM who professed undying love for me used to tell me, "I can't concentrate on anything at home because I see your face all the time. It's getting more and more difficult to hide the fact that I'm in love with another woman." But hide it he did, reiterating my point that words are easy and totally vacuous. It's action that talks!

As part of the MM's "wife not understanding him" speech, he may tell you that he isn't sleeping with her (see chapter ten, "I'm Not Sleeping with My Wife"), and in the beginning you *may* believe him (although you might not care either way at that early stage). But the deeper your relationship becomes, the more it will start bothering you. If you do believe him (foolish!), then you will trust that he is not lying to you. Because if you can't have trust between you, what's the point of anything, right?

You may even begin to feel sorry for him, thinking he must be so unhappy at home. Therefore, when he comes to you, you find yourself overcompensating in order to make him feel happy and loved—and to make him want to come back for more.

✎ **NOTE TO MISTRESSES:** *Don't!* Remember that he *does* have a choice. And his choice is to stay with her—period. And also think about *you*. You'll be the one hurting when he takes that shower and gets dressed in the middle of the night to go back to his wife, leaving you alone in bed.

✎ **HYGIENE NOTE:** The MM will never leave to go home without taking a shower first (or at least very thoroughly washing his vitals).

The longer you allow the affair to go on, the more you will get acclimated to being in it, and the level of pain I've mentioned will become the norm to you. He will keep trying to assure you that he is only with his wife because of the children and that he would never be with her otherwise. That'll gradually wear thin (although note to self: I must admit it took a while to wear thin on me).

✎ **NOTE TO MISTRESSES:** I'm assuming here that your MM has children. Otherwise, why in the hell are you having an affair with a loser who wants to keep two women going without being able to use his kids as an excuse?

🖎 **FURTHER NOTE TO MISTRESSES:** I'm also assuming that you care for your MM (with children) because my comments are directed to those of you who love/like/or are at least fond of him to some degree. If that's not the case and you're just using him, that's totally fine, but this chapter may not be for you.

The typical MM and father will make out to you that his children are the most important thing in the whole world to him, and it's their happiness and stability that are always at top of his list.

🖎 **NOTE:** Well, we know *that* can't be true, or he wouldn't be putting his penis in a woman who isn't their mother, now would he!

Depending on the kids' ages, he will milk this "importance" thing. If they're young, he may tell you that he couldn't possibly leave his wife, as she would never cope and he hasn't yet bonded with the kids properly. (Note to self: is he too busy bonding with his mistress, perchance?) His concern will be that if he did leave her she might stop him from seeing his children.

🖎 **NOTE TO ALL:** That's what courts of law and alimony are for. It *is* doable, and many people manage to make new lives, which go on to include healthy relationships with their children (sometimes even better ones). So cowardly, pussy-whipped MMs, please wake up!

If the kids are older, say in their teens, he may tell you that he couldn't possibly leave his wife until the kids are safely in college or university, so that they have stability until they leave home (you're looking at the ripe old age of about eighteen years old per kid there).

🖎 **BOREDOM NOTE:** This is a long time to wait, ladies, especially when you know he will never leave his wife, as there will always be another bigger and better excuse waiting around the corner.

If you're with an older MM and his kids are already grown and married, it will be a case of him waiting to become (or having just become) a grandparent. Therefore he couldn't possibly "upset" his grown son or daughter in this scenario.

🖎 **NOTE TO MISTRESSES:** As you listen to this tripe of him not wanting to hurt or damage the people and the relationships he has around him, always remember that he finds it easy to hurt *you* constantly, by keeping you a secret and forcing you to accept the fact he is with someone else if you wish to carry on seeing him. (Note the passive-aggressive behavior from him there!)

The MM will use a never-ending list of excuses regarding the children in order to convince himself, and you, that he has to keep his situation as it is and that he and his wife have to stay as they are. *Only the strong ones leave.* The rest do not want to face the reality of what they have created.

✎ **NOTE TO MISTRESSES:** By putting all their energy into their kids and "living for them," an unhappy husband and wife can avoid confronting the fact that their marriage is completely broken. Their kids become a Band-Aid on their relationship.

As you can see, there are a plethora of reasons, which I prefer to call *excuses*, and more often than not *lies*, as to why the MM "can't" leave his wife but why he wants, and constantly justifies, having an affair. But believe me, sisters (and these are some of the truest words I will ever speak to you), if he really *was* in a bad relationship with his wife, he wouldn't physically or mentally be able to be with her. And if he had *really* fallen in love with you (as much as he might be telling you he has), he would have the overwhelming desire to make the lifestyle changes required in order to make you happy and not run the risk of losing you.

In addition, if he had any self-respect or concern for the quality of his own life, he would make these changes for himself more than anyone else, so let's just leave it at that.

✎ **REMINDER NOTE TO MISTRESSES:** Men who cheat are literally men on the lookout for something better, men who are keeping their options open. You can see why this type of man will never commit to you nor leave his wife for you. Either way, he will be completely noncommittal.

A bad marriage can be likened to a really bad job. You know it's not for you; you hate going there every day; but you know you have to until you find something better. You know you want and deserve more, but at the moment it's all you've got. You don't invest quality time in your colleagues. You don't read any of the company manuals and information you should, as you know you are going to be out of there the first chance you land something better. Basically you don't show interest in anything you can get away with not having to, because what's the point pretending your heart is there when it's not? Do you see my point?

Throughout the book, I have touched upon the excuses an MM will feed you as to the reasons why he "can't" leave his wife for you—from blackmail issues to financial issues to his children—even when the children have already left home!

I want to share an example of the "older child" excuse. A wonderfully sassy friend of mine, let's call her Miranda, was until recently having an affair with a much older man. He stipulated that he couldn't leave his wife (even though she apparently had not understood him for the last forty years of their marriage), due to the fact that his youngest son, who was only seventeen, would lose respect for him. (His other four kids were grown and had left home.)

Apparently the worry began to cause this MM some health problems and tugged so much at his already dodgy "angina heartstrings" that he felt he had to bring his affair to a close. Even though he professed that Miranda was absolutely the love of his life and that he thought about her all the time (the usual diatribe of stuff we like to hear in the beginning, but that pisses us off in the end).

Miranda and "Mr. Angina" had been dating on and off for about twenty years. (Can you believe? Strike two!) And just take a guess at which one is the millionaire, owns many successful businesses, has a large family, beautiful home, grandchildren, and constantly travels the world for business and pleasure? And which is the sad, lonely, fabulously attractive person missing her companion, sitting in a beautifully over-furnished, perfectly maintained one-bedroom apartment in Beverly Hills? A place she can't really afford, which he *never once* offered to help her with—even though he *so* could've afforded to. Especially as the scales were unfairly balanced in her favor…coupled with the fact that he was happy enough to use her place as a secret love nest as often as it suited him!

✎ **WAKE-UP NOTE:** Mistresses, this is a perfect example of an MM being allowed to "swan in and swan out" of your life and your home, to suit himself, reaping the benefits of a goodhearted mistress along the way.

So, Mr. Angina's "traits" eventually shone through—cowardly, shallow, and *tight as hell*—and ultimately he was willing to lose the alleged love of his life in order to stay in his vacuous martial situation. *Loser!*

✎ **CHURLISH NOTE:** The fact that Miranda told me he had erectile dysfunction made me beam from ear to ear. He had hurt my friend—so what goes around really does "come" around (or maybe *not* in his case!).

Another good "lifestyle excuse" you might hear from the MM, so that he doesn't have to make changes at home, is the one about him wanting to leave his wife but not being able to because it would ruin him financially. This can only be used by moderately wealthy to very rich men—or those waiting for a health insurance payout.

✎ **NOTE TO MISTRESSES OF A WEALTHY MM:** If you decide to accept the "financially crippling" reason as an excuse for him not to leave, make sure he is spoiling you BIG TIME in return. You should want for nothing with this type of MM. After all, whatever he spends on you will be far less than the amount his wife would use to turn him into the financial paraplegic he's so scared of becoming!

The next and final excuse (for now) is one I hadn't personally come across before. It was presented to a mistress friend of mine last year: "My wife is dying of cancer, so I can't leave her at the moment!" (Sisters, I'm not even going to *go* there. All I would say is, as with everything else we've discussed, seek proof and do your DD wisely.)

RECAP NOTES TO MISTRESSES:

- Remember that his wife usually does understand him. He just says she doesn't to make you feel sorry for him and to get you into bed. He is really just bored and fancies something new.
- Don't believe a word your MM says in general.
- Find out if he is a player or if you (and his wife) are the *only* women he's sleeping with (even though he'll tell you that *you* are the only woman, as he isn't sleeping with his wife...so just "note," but ignore and dismiss, that one).
- If you do doubt his extra extramarital activities, make sure you practice safe sex and self-protection.
- Always remember, mistresses, that you are allowing him to have his cake and eat it too. Make sure you're getting some cake as well!

Mistresses, at the end of the day, you will go along with all of this...*until you don't.* And you need to reach that point of disillusionment by yourself, not because people tell you to. All you can hope for is that the ones who tried to warn you off being involved with an MM are still around to pick up the pieces when you eventually reach the same verdict they did, months (or sadly, sometimes years) later.

✎ **BONUS NOTE TO WIVES:** Here are some common signs to look for if you think your husband is having an affair. And remember, the biggest telltale sign of whether your spouse is cheating is that you're asking yourself that question in the first place.

- He speaks in a low voice on the phone or hangs up quickly.
- He has an unusual "glow" about him.
- He wants to try new sexual positions with you.
- He suddenly wants to help you do his laundry.
- He spends an excessive amount of time on the computer after you've gone to bed.

chapter 7

For Richer or Poorer

The Mistress Makes an MM Happy,
Yet the Wife Benefits from All Her Hard Work

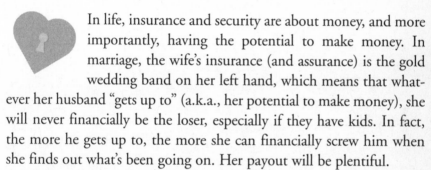 In life, insurance and security are about money, and more importantly, having the potential to make money. In marriage, the wife's insurance (and assurance) is the gold wedding band on her left hand, which means that whatever her husband "gets up to" (a.k.a., her potential to make money), she will never financially be the loser, especially if they have kids. In fact, the more he gets up to, the more she can financially screw him when she finds out what's been going on. Her payout will be plentiful.

Whether they end up getting divorced is between them, but that gold band is quite literally her cash register (do I hear a *ka-ching* in the background?), and the children are her escrow fund! The wealthier the man, the bigger her dividend. It's that simple.

✎ **NOTE TO MARRIED MEN:** You have no chance of winning in this situation (this goes for long-term partners and common-law husbands too). You will get screwed over and over—literally and metaphorically. Is it really worth it, gentlemen?

In a typical marriage, the driving force and *modus operandi* for wives is usually money, and for their husbands it's usually sex. Each one wants large quantities of both (or at least what they feel they're entitled to), and unfortunately some marriages become a war when the two collaterals are bartered out beyond all reasonable proportion. And rather than address what is actually wrong in the relationship, the wife often just takes away the sex.

✎ **NOTE TO WIVES:** This is not such a smart move in the big picture!

For the record, I'm not talking about *all* marriages, *all* wives, or *all* husbands—just most! I know there are always exceptions to the rule. I'm making generalizations—observations based on facts gathered through my research and personal experience.

If the marriage is breaking down, then the more money the MM makes, the more likely the wife will be to ensure that she enjoys her lifestyle—over and above enjoying her husband and trying to make him happy, leaving him a very real emotional void to somehow fill.

✎ **NOTE:** Hence, the mistress is alive and well, and her "position" will never be redundant, as she provides too vital a service to the community!

Many marriages can become an upward struggle, a war of power and control: the husband using his money to gain power and control over his wife, and the wife using her vagina to maintain power and *financial* control over her husband. (Isn't it amazing how the woman's side of things somehow always comes back to the rudiments of being a hooker?)

If the husband is successful, and chooses to exist in a bad marriage because it suits him, he will keep giving and giving to his wife in order to keep her at bay. If she's equally unhappy, she will keep taking and taking. The division between them will grow. They will become disparate *and* desperate.

✎ **NOTE TO BUDGET-CONSCIOUS MISTRESSES:** If the MM happens to have a mistress who is making him *very* happy, he may be inclined to allow his wife more funds than usual in order to keep her busier, happier, and more distant—affording him the space he requires to be with his other woman *more* often!

Think about it, mistresses (and I'm assuming you're intelligent women here). Would you ever invest so much of yourself, your valuable time, and your energy into any other project in your life—business or personal—if you downright knew someone else was getting so much more out of it than you were? Could you ever be comfortable with another person (the wife in this case) reaping the benefits of your conscientious hard work? All that tenacious handiwork you're putting into your MM (quite literally), all that good work for which you'll *never* get credit or recognition!

✎ **NOTE:** Could the well-practiced, *smooth* hand of a mistress be looked upon as the ghostwriter of the MM's marriage? Could the mistress be the anonymous person who is actually determining the story and outcome of their marital longevity? A ghost*wifer* perhaps!

So now, back to the "loyalty rewards program." Imagine you work at a city firm, and you're faced with the prospect of somebody else getting all of the "life security" and company perks that *you* should be in line for, based on the exemplary hard work and overtime you're putting into the job. You would never entertain the idea of being in such a role, would you?

Yet that's exactly what you're doing as a mistress. Your MM's wife isn't putting much effort into her "job"—she *can't* be. She isn't working overtime to make your MM happy. If she was, then he wouldn't be with you in the first place. So why should you feel guilty, mistresses? There's no need. It's not your fault, after all.

✎ **NOTE TO MISTRESSES (AND WIVES) OF WEALTHY MEN:** An unhappy, multi-multi-millionaire married man (an "MMMMM") recently told me, "All the money in the world doesn't mean a thing if a man isn't happy, and a man isn't happy if he isn't getting laid!" The man in question was genuinely not into hookers, as is the case with so many men. Therefore he had a mistress. (There must be some sort of ironic joke or comparison to be inserted here!)

Having an affair makes home life much more bearable for the MM because it gives him an outlet for his unhappiness—in the form of something and someone to look forward to seeing. A retreat, for want of a better word.

The happier his affair and his mistress's attentions make him, the nicer he'll appear to act at home. This ultimately makes for a far more pleasant environment for his wife to live in, compared to his pre-mistress mood.

✎ **NOTE TO INQUISITIVE MISTRESSES:** Just out of curiosity, I wonder what the wife attributes his newfound happiness to (and if she even notices?).

He'll no longer have those annoying tensions and stresses he used to suffer when his wife wasn't trying to meet his emotional needs— because he'll no longer care.

✎ **COLLATERAL NOTE:** Mistress or no mistress, an MM will always have sex with his wife if she instigates it. Always! This is because he is so used to her *not* wanting him and refusing his attentions that it will make him feel "wanted" and "husbandly" to have to perform, as no man likes the rejection that MMs suffer in the marital bed. More to the point, he will feel it's his due and will want to collect what he is owed! The wife will feel that she has done him a humongous self-sacrificial favor, believing it will keep him satisfied for a good few months. *Ha—whatever!*

An MM once told me that, for him, having an affair made things so much easier at home when performing his husbandly and fatherly duties. He was no longer trying to make his relationship work on a romantic level. (In other words, he wasn't under pressure anymore.) He said that although nothing had actually *changed* and they still went about things as they always had, the difference was that he had emotionally "left the building."

Hence the more content an MM becomes, the more his wife's dreary married life will be enhanced by his new cheery disposition— while, conversely, the ghostwifer's "life of a mistress" might well be drained by jealousy, longing, angst, and insecurity.

✎ **NOTE TO MISTRESSES:** You do realize that you're actually helping them *both*, don't you? You're providing a form of free marriage counseling, if you will.

The longer your affair goes on, the more pangs of guilt the MM could begin to feel toward his wife (never toward you, though, because he's "never promised you anything," right?). And so, once again, the more liberal he becomes with his cash where his wife is concerned—if he has it to splash out with in the first place, of course (and if he doesn't have it, there is always debt!).

He may increase her housekeeping allowance, or he may pony up the money required for a downpayment on that new car she's been eyeing, and so on.

🚗 **VEHICULAR NOTE TO MISTRESSES:** Just out of interest, what car are *you* driving these days?

Basically the MM will do whatever he has to in order to keep the equilibrium ticking along at home, so that he's able to carry on seeing you secretly.

Sisters, the more experienced you become at being the mistress, the more you'll feel cheated and chagrined at being the one who is loving the MM, listening to him constantly download his woes and stresses, and generally enhancing his well-being and happiness. Quite probably you're the one *doing* it all—and getting nothing. Unlike his wife, who is quite probably *getting* it all—for doing nothing!

And it is at times like these, in the face of adversity, that a mistress must ask herself not what the wife can do for her husband, but what her husband can do for his mistress!

✎ **NOTE:** Many MMs have the notion that their mistress has life all sorted and wants for nothing. Therefore, he will hardly ever ask if she needs anything. This could be due to the fact that the typically unhappy MM is *so* used to associating giving his money to a woman he "doesn't love" that he may not think to pass any moola in the direction of the one he *does* "love." It can also be due to the strong independent streak most mistresses automatically tend to possess—and exude—as the by-product of being an SUW.

It's already bad enough that you're doing an outstanding job and someone else is reaping the rewards, but on top of that, you have to "grin and bear it" as you watch your MM leave you to go back to his other life, cutting off contact with you for the duration. It's painful enough for the mistress to know that she has helped him go back to a life she hates him being in, but sending him back as a better, happier person is even more gut-wrenching. (Damn, it's hard for a mistress!)

✎ **NOTE TO MISTRESSSES:** Some MMs view a mistress as their own personal marriage counselor and hooker all in one. I can understand that theory. After all, he gets a weekly fix of free therapy—and some regular sex sessions too. After which he's "good to go" (right back to his wife!).

So, back to my earlier question, ladies: Would you *really* contemplate investing yourself, your care, and your time into any other situation or area in your life where you put out so much and settle for so little in return? If you're honest with yourself, you know the answer is *no*—the hell you would!

✎ **NOTE TO MISTRESSES WHO BECAME WEALTHY AND INDEPENDENT THROUGH AN AFFAIR WITH AN MM:** Well done! I commend you for getting there. I suggest you write a book to explain the shortest possible route the rest of us can take.

Moving on, mistresses… Let's assume you know the score by now and the affair is working for you just as much as it is for him. If that is the case, you should at least examine why you're in the affair and know from the outset what you want from it. That way you can deal with things accordingly and engineer what *you* want your unavailable man to bring to your empty table (with the place setting for one).

Ask yourself questions like: Do you want a life with this guy? Are you falling in love with him?

✎ **NOTE:** Do *not* fall in love with him! I already told you that. This man is not your boyfriend, nor your husband, and he never will be. So what on earth is the point of being in love with him? You can like him, sure. But love? *No way!*

Maybe you're lonely, and your MM is the best you can get at the moment. Or perhaps you're in it just for a bit of fun. Maybe a promotion or a salary increase, if your MM happens to be your boss. Perhaps this affair is just a fling to get over a previous lover. Or if your MM is wealthy, you might have decided that your affair will provide you with a better lifestyle than you're currently experiencing. Whatever the reasons for your affair, if you know which road you're on, it makes it a hell of a lot easier for you to "drive the bus," so to speak, to ensure that things go *your* way.

Undoubtedly at some point you'll find yourself comparing how your MM treats you with how you perceive he treats his wife. It's only natural. Unless you know her personally, which is risky, you can only base your critical analysis and critique on the financial information he has shared with you, especially regarding his wife and her possessions.

✎ **MATERIALISTIC NOTE TO MISTRESSES:** If the results of the comparison seem stacked in *her* favor, it will be somewhat depressing for you. However, it could be a good wake-up call as to the best way to move forward (or move him out of your life—which is better, if he's not adding much fiscal value).

✎ **NOTE:** In some parts of the world where having more than one wife (and a few concubines) is legal, the MM treats all his women *equally*.

My dear friend Miranda would predictably call me every week in tears, telling me of the wonderful things her MM, Mr. Angina, was doing with his wife. (He was obviously giving Miranda only the bare bones of information, but she was glamorizing it to suit her pain, as so many mistresses do.) Her MM's activities included taking his wife on a three-week vacation to Europe, whilst he professed having *no* available time to see Miranda before leaving on his travels. Although to be fair to the man, he did say he wanted to see her *so badly*, because he did love her so very much.

"HAVING AN *Affair?*"

✎ **NOTE TO READERS:** And you wonder why I'm cynical!

Miranda, who was very lonely at the time, sadly hung on his every word. She made excuses to me about why he had to take his wife away on holiday, even insisting that she was sure he didn't really want to—just that he *had to*. But here's the thing—he, like all other MMs, couldn't do this stuff if it was *so* unbearable. It would be impossible to hold himself together, even for the sake of the kids. It was obvious (to me anyway) that his relationship with his wife was nowhere near as bad as he tried to make out it was to poor, believing Miranda.

✎ **NOTE TO ALL MISTRESSES:** That's the real truth in all this. Most of these marriages are nowhere near as rough and rocky as the guy tells you they are. Sadly, the husband and wife's loveless existence becomes all they know and acts as their safety net. They may fool around separately, and they may *think* they want out, but unless things are truly "plate-smashingly" unbearable at home, if push came to shove, ninety-nine percent of them would stay with each other and keep their situation as it is.

The end of the Miranda tale is that her MM promised he would find time to see her when he returned from his three-week family trip and that he really wanted her to know just how much he would be thinking of her while he was away (oh, P-L-E-A-S-E!). He told her all the things he wanted to do with her, and to her, when he got back *(blah blah blah)*.

✎ **NOTE TO MMs:** "Thinking" doesn't do anything to enrich your mistress's life in any way. All it does is help *you* get by when you're with your wife but wishing you were with your mistress. (PS: Wishing doesn't achieve anything either, guys!)

He promised to call her before he flew, but he must've been thinking of her so much that he clean forgot. The result being that she had a terrible three weeks compared to his no doubt pleasant sojourn. She was daily committing mental suicide as to why he couldn't have just found five minutes to call her to say good-bye. She missed him terribly, though she felt angry at herself for missing him, and she hoped like crazy that he would call while he was away—if only to explain why he hadn't called before he left. At least then she could vent her anger and disappointment to him before he got back, and hopefully upset the rest of his trip in the process!

Those three weeks felt like a hellish three months and dragged by cruelly, whereas his long vacation probably flew by way too fast for him and his wife.

The bastard didn't call one time while he was away. That's how much he missed her, and just how awful it was being with his wife for three long weeks! Again, do you see my point now about words being vacuous, but actions speaking volumes? Miranda had no option but to sweat it out and wait for her "beloved," which made her a nervous wreck and very bitter by the time he got back.

Mistresses often experience the feeling of being second best—and bitterness too. It goes with the territory, even although your MM will tell you that you're *never* second best in his eyes.

✎ **NOTE TO MISTRESSES:** But who cares about *his* eyes? It's how you see things that matters.

You will also experience the pain of low self-esteem and acute lack of self-worth the longer your affair goes on, especially at times like these, when your MM goes on holiday with his wife and family.

✎ **NOTE:** If you care about your MM (remember not to love him, or you are doomed!), then all of these feelings will go hand in hand with being a mistress, I'm afraid. Watch out for them! You must refuse to allow yourself to give way to these emotions, as they are destructive and will eat into your soul like a cancer if you let them.

On top of these debilitating emotions, some mistresses may also exhibit bouts of erratic behavior from time to time, ranging from abusive verbal tirades and threats, to sending hurtful text messages and e-mails telling him you never want to see him again—*unless he tells his wife about you.*

This is a normal reaction, and there's no need to worry—you aren't sick. Your behavior is based on your feeling of low importance in your

MM's life, believing you come in last on his inventory of priorities and to-do lists. These already *intense* sentiments will be further mixed with some acute jealousy and uncertainty, finished off with a twist of loneliness and despair (and often fueled by alcohol!).

✎ **NOTE TO MISTRESSES:** He will dismiss these outbursts as you being "a crazy person," "a mad, unbalanced woman," or a "borderline alcoholic" (all the things he is no doubt helping you turn into, but will never take responsibility for). Ultimately, your behavior will work in his favor, as your perceived instability and quasi-mental sickness will act as another reason why he can't leave his wife for you (i.e., you're a madwoman and he'd be nervous to introduce his children to you). Trust me, ladies, I've heard it all!

🔑 **TIP FOR EMOTIONAL, BORDERLINE-ALCOHOLIC MISTRESSES:** Don't drink and dial (nor text or e-mail). You will *so* regret it the next morning!

If you have reached this point and feel the need to make such a cry for a reaction from him, I would imagine he's been lying to you for some time now, leading you to believe he was going to tell his wife about you, and make a plan for the two of you to be together.

✎ **NOTE:** You need to talk to him about this, as things (for you) will only get progressively worse, not better. Talk it through with him before you're tempted to do something silly, like upsetting his house of cards in order to prove your point (and you know what I mean by that!).

If he's trying to buy more time with you (for sex) but has no intention of telling his wife that they are done, he may try to suppress your temper and outbursts for a while with a few baubles and trinkets, hoping to make everything peachy again. Don't be lured into the trap (but do take the baubles and trinkets!). Still, know that you have to deal with your brewing emotions, because if he *isn't* going to leave his wife, you're going to end up angrier and angrier the next time—and who knows what you'll do then?

✎ **NOTE TO TEMPORARILY INSANE MISTRESSES:** Try to curb things early on. Seriously. Or you might get so depressed about the whole situation that you end up calling his wife and telling her everything. (Reminder tip: *Don't drink and dial!*)

✎ **NOTE TO MMs:** If that happens, and your mistress decides to steal your home number from your mobile phone to have a little chat with your wife, you may wish you had taken the time to be a tad more concerned about your mistress's feelings and mental welfare along the way. Although remember my point about "wishing" not doing you any good whatsoever, gentlemen? Once that fuse has been lit, you can't stop the explosion from happening!

Let's move on now, ladies, to the real point of this chapter: the benefits you can and should expect from your MM during an affair. Because if you choose to subject yourself to the intense heartache of being emotionally involved with a man who lives his life with another woman, you should logically be getting something of benefit to yourself out of it, don't you think?

I'll be discussing the category of middle- to upper-wealthy MMs only, as I do not see any benefits whatsoever to having an affair with a poor man. Why on earth would you want to position yourself in such a dead-end relationship with an unavailable man if you aren't benefiting from the arrangement at least as much—*or more*—than he is? (Sorry, but I just don't get that one!) Which ultimately means an MM *has* to have money in order to facilitate more than one relationship—it's just a fact!

✎ **NOTE TO WELL-HEELED MISTRESSES OF MONIED MEN:** It's amazing how a swanky little Gucci bag, a pair of Jimmy Choos, or some snazzy Roberto Cavalli pants can alleviate that pain of missing him (well, temporarily)—at least until you become so accustomed to wearing fabulous shoes that the novelty wears thin. Be careful that you're not selling your (married) *manmade* "soles" short in order to have the best wardrobe in town—but the emptiest bed on the block.

"HAVING AN *Affair?*"

The beginning of your affair will be an exciting time, full of clandestine telephone calls, and illicit liaisons anywhere and everywhere (perhaps all over the world if you pick the right guy). You will want to see each other whenever humanly possible, and you'll both, no doubt, do some crazy things in order to make that happen.

✎ **UTILITY BILL NOTE TO MISTRESSES:** Let *him* make most of the phone calls so that you don't get stuck with a huge bill (particularly if he lives in another country or another state). Even if he says he'll pay your bill when it arrives, don't let it run up, because if your affair comes to an abrupt end (or he gets hit by a bus), the responsibility will be on you. Plus, it will make you feel cheap (not good for an already sensitive mistress) if you have to present him with a bill. It's far better to avoid such things by just putting the onus on him beforehand.

$ EXPENSE NOTE: The same rule applies to *all* flights, travel, and out-of-pocket expenses and incidentals for the times when he wants to see you or have you meet him somewhere. If you're traveling the world with him, then you already know he can afford these extras.

You should expect to enjoy being wined, dined, and generally indulged at the best restaurants all over town, experiencing gastronomic delights and fine wines. You will hopefully get to stay at some of the best hotels in the world. (*Not* the Best Western or the Holiday Inn. Ladies, *please*. Those hotels are for wives, not you!) Basically, you should be getting the best out of everything that he and your affair has to offer, right? I don't see how anyone on earth could dispute *that* statement!

✎ **WORLDLY EDUCATIONAL NOTE TO MISTRESSES:** When eating out, make sure you sample as many of the best wines your MM can afford—or rather that his company AMEX card can afford—making a mental note of the different names, labels, vineyards, and so on. Constantly learn all you can about the finer things in life, especially if he is sophisticated. He can teach you much that will benefit you in future relationships and in your life in general. Remember, knowledge is power—*it doesn't matter how you learn it!*

In return, be sure to give constant attention to your MM, because let's face it, it must be pretty boring going home to his wife after having spent the evening with you!

✎ **NOTE TO YOUNGER MISTRESSES:** If your MM is a lot older than you, he might be relieved to go home to his wife for a rest after being with you, as I doubt he can keep up with you *every* night.

Let him spoil you completely, and I mean *really* let him. Don't tell him, "Oh, you don't have to do that," because you know what? Yes, he *does* have to! Use some words of encouragement to induce his generosity if you think he's being a bit slow on the uptake.

☛ **STERN NOTE TO MISTRESSES:** Don't do something pathetic, like falling in love with him and then losing the plot on all this!

And by *spoiling*, we're talking flowers, jewelry, holidays, and shopping, perhaps a little car to run around in—whatever you *know* he can afford. Because trust me, he will be spending a lot more on his wife than on you—forever mindful that he needs to keep the deception at the family home going so that he is able to come out and play with you.

✎ **NOTE:** Remember, though, you are not *just* a plaything for him whenever he feels like seeing you. You too need and deserve nice things to play with, and in, when he's not around. You need nice things even more if he requests that you be exclusive to him. And if you agree to that request, the stakes are immediately upped in your favor. If you do say you'll be exclusive to him, for God's sake, *don't mean it* or practice it, or you will never find that Mr. Right (the one you've stopped looking for while being attached to your MM!).

If your MM is tight with his luxuries, which is so unattractive, talk to him about it. Tell him you need a bit of help with something or other. Make up a little reason why you need some help, as a test, early on into your "arrangement." Many of the women I interviewed backed this one up wholeheartedly. (Sadly, those who didn't were still in denial or *so* desperate to be loved that they would be martyrs for any MM that looked twice at them.)

One non-martyr mistress told her MM that her bag had been stolen and she'd lost her wallet, phone, the lot. He felt so sorry for her that he replaced everything, above and beyond what she had actually "lost." He went on to have a good run for his money with her, as he had proved himself from the start. She told me that some of the others she'd "road tested" didn't act quite so generously, and she had unceremoniously dumped them.

✎ **PERSONAL COMMENT NOTE:** I like straight-talking women who know what they want and go after it. The Judge Judys of the affair world, perhaps! After all, life is way too short to be in a holding pattern.

Examples like that are sensible little tests, ladies (and another way of doing some invaluable DD), to help you understand whether he is in the affair only for short haul fornication (SHF) or whether he actually really cares an ounce about you and your well-being.

✎ **REMINDER NOTE TO MISTRESSES:** Never forget, you are choosing to be with an MM rather than being with an *available* man who would be reliable and be "there for you" whenever you needed him (in an honest and real relationship). You would perhaps even be carving a future together. Your MM is denying you that, although his future is mapped out for sure. But more importantly, mistresses, you are denying yourself a normal—better?—future.

I recommend that you use any means you see fit and feel comfortable with, in order to find out whether your MM would be there for you if you ever needed him to step up to the table—if, in fact, he has a desire to invest in you and *your* happiness or only in his own!

Now, you will obviously need a "safe house" in which to meet, in order to carry out the affair—unless you plan to meet at hotels all the time (and don't settle for that if it's his choice but not something *you* want).

For Richer or Poorer
The Mistress Makes an MM Happy, Yet the Wife Benefits from All Her Hard Work

✎ **LODGINGS NOTE:** Hotels will be essential if you, the mistress, happen to be a married woman and not an SUW at all!

If you're a single woman involved in a *serious* affair, then your big, strong hero of an MM should really be doing something about providing a roof over your head in order to be able to conduct the affair he wants to have with you.

✎ **NOTE OF COMPARISON:** Even hookers are mindful to include their accommodations overhead in their rates!

Let's face it, your MM is providing a roof over his wife's lovely head (a roof he will *say* he doesn't want to live under), so why on earth can't he do the same for you? What's so shocking about that suggestion—especially if he can afford it? If he's wealthy, he will have certain standards he'll want to adhere to and will hardly want to conduct his adulterous business in a shoddy studio apartment (if that's where you happen to live) or in view of a roommate's prying eyes.

✎ **A NOTE OF EXPERIENCE TO MISTRESSES LIVING IN A SHODDY APARTMENT:** On reflection, he may in fact be okay with downgrading to trysts at your place, especially if he only sees your "agreement" as a means to regular ejaculation, rather than nesting for the future, and especially if he isn't the most generous of men. It could well suit him not to have to part with any more of his hard-earned cash and thus not create suspicion from his wife when she's doing the accounts. By coming to your place, he isn't expending or outlaying anything, and therefore won't have to answer those oh-so-nagging questions about sudden credit card bills or bank transfers to leasing agents. (This type of MM will make the best of any location and will refer to your place as cute—*as it suits him to.*)

Wake up, mistresses. There is no chance in hell you that should go along with this one. Especially if your affair is deemed "serious" on both sides. If he professes to love you and *not* his wife (and you choose to believe him), then give me one good reason why he can't treat you both equally? Why should he be providing a far better lifestyle for her than you? (And please don't give me the "because of the kids" line here, as it's *you* who is giving him more of what he needs, not her.)

I met and interviewed an American woman at an airport bar who shared an experience with me that actually summed up this subject quite nicely. She told me she had joined Match.com hoping to meet a single man. She unfortunately attracted a married one, who obviously chose to leave that little detail *out* of his profile in order to attract an unknowing partner.

✎ **NOTE TO WIVES:** Remember what I said about him being on the computer late in the evening?

He had the audacity to get as far as taking her out on a date. During the conversation, she caught him out and (quite reasonably) suggested that he should get his wife to "service" him rather than asking *her* out on a date, as it was the wife's bills he was paying, not hers.

He got angry with this woman, so she said, "Don't get angry at me! Get angry at your wife for shutting you down sexually. If she's that great, why isn't she sleeping with you? And why get mad at me? You should be getting mad at your wife, not some other woman!" Needless to say, they didn't see each other again.

Sisters, SUWs, and mistresses collectively, if you're already happily settled in your abode, it's not shoddy, and you don't have a roommate to pry, then at least let him help you with your upkeep (and engineer that he does). Things like some help with the rent, buying a few items for the house, or just taking care of a few bills will act as an extremely nice gesture from him. (Never say no—even if it's just out of spite, so that it's less housekeeping money into his wife's wallet that week!)

✎ **NOTE TO MISTRESSES:** Never be out-of-pocket for your MM, even if you can afford it. Don't let him swan in and swan out of your life and your home with no obligation or contribution whatsoever while reaping all the benefits from you. Teach your MM the fine art of give and take, not *just* take and take!

✎ **NOTE TO (NOVICE) MISTRESSES:** During the love cocktail stage, you won't feel so cynical and mercenary with regards to your

MM, but as you progress down the path of your affair, *you definitely will.*

Plus—and depending on how serious your affair becomes—if you *do* create a secret home together, you will ultimately be developing a stronger bond between the two of you. You will have "your place" in common, which will make him all the more attached to you and all the more comfortable in the relationship you share. Rule of thumb is that it should make it harder for him to leave you, to be away from you and "your place" (a.k.a. his second home).

✎ **NOTE TO MISTRESSES ON A MISSION:** If you really like this guy, and if you're trying to get him—to leave his wife—then acquiring a place together (that you choose and he pays for) will add an extra string to your bow. You will become like a second wife (although the quality of the sex and the conversation will be far better). If he likes the home you create together, it will be a double bonus for you, as it will make it twice as hard for him to constantly leave you to go back to his husbandly responsibilities. (Plus you get to live rent-free—cool or what!)

Become his best friend, not just his lover. Be everything that his wife obviously isn't, namely spontaneous, interested in his work, sexy at all times, and *ready* for sex whenever and wherever. That'll be your winning combo.

✎ **NOTE TO MISTRESSES:** If you make him feel attractive and loved and also become his confidante, he will always come back for more.

We know sex is easy to come by for men (especially successful ones), but the bond, the friendship, and the intimacy, which can make things like fantasies and games such fun, as well as the reciprocation of mutual attraction—these things are very hard to come by in a relationship and very hard to give up when you have actually enjoyed them with someone. He obviously came to you in the first place because of being unhappy at home, and due to his wife being inadequate to him in some way, so bank that one and try to keep being all the things he pursued you for from the get-go.

A mistress will typically live as, and be perceived as, an SUW to the outside world. Mistresses can never be too vocal about who they're having an affair with, not only because it's a stigma and people will be quick to judge, but also in case anyone knows him and busts his secret (although quite frankly, why we would protect a liar I don't know).

If he is high profile, then you really *can't* tell anyone without—literally—losing sleep at night. High profile is fun, and all that paparazzi dodging can be excellent for the libido, but it's a nightmare if your affair is discovered! You will be painted as the loose woman with no morals whilst he nonchalantly stands at the gate of his country home with his family gathered around him, "supporting" him. He will be holding his wife's hand, and she will be "sticking by him" and "talking things through with him" (remember my opening statement about her wedding band being her financial security?). The main thing she will be "talking through" with him will be the amount of compensation she is expecting based on what he has spent on his mistress during the affair.

Only you will know your MM and what he can and can't afford (although he may lie and defraud you on that score). He might find it hard to account for extra outgoings and to explain to his wife where exactly the money that he is spending on you and your relationship is going.

✎ **NOTE TO MISTRESSES:** Tough! That's totally his problem, not yours! Don't get involved in how they manage their day-to-day finances and expenses as a couple. I'm sure he'll be able to massage a few "extras" into the regular bills that land in their mailbox.

What he *is* able to spend on you will depend largely on what he earns versus what disposable income he has on hand. For a lot of MMs having an affair, the credit card bills take some explaining to the wife, but he has to use credit cards because large amounts of cash withdrawn from the (joint) account wouldn't do either. That would be even harder to explain!

✎ **NOTE TO MMs:** This is what company credit cards, expense accounts, and offshore bank accounts were created for.

If he is a big shot businessman, financial restrictions may not be so prevalent, because normally a guy who rakes in a fortune will usually siphon off some cash to play with, without his wife knowing. Plus, with the trappings of pension funds, bonuses, and offshore bank accounts for these types of high-flyers, she will be far less privy to his financial arrangements. Only you will be able to judge his financial situation and whether he is a generous person, but you should try and do this from the beginning, so you will at least know where you stand (and what shoes you should budget for!).

If he happens to say that he finds it difficult to treat you generously because his wife takes care of the finances, don't accept it. He doesn't find it difficult to lie to her about where he is when he's having sex with you, does he? So let him find a way to spoil you as well. Where there's a will there's a way—and if he can't find one, then move on to somebody who can.

✎ **NOTE:** Never allow yourself to be an unpaid hooker for your MM. He will let you if you're not careful, as sex was the main reason he came to you in the first place. Why should a mistress make it easy for him to have his cake and eat it too? Unless she also is stuffing her face with as big a slice as his wife is consuming (and without putting on the same amount of calories, of course!).

Why am I so adamant about this? I'll tell you why. Because his wife will have *everything* she needs; he will continually make sure of that (and, in fact, probably overcompensate her whilst he is having the affair) to keep her happy and to help eliminate any trouble.

✎ **NOTE TO MISTRESSES:** Remember what I said earlier: "The wife will *always* have security through her association with her husband." *Do you have any?*

She will have a roof over her head and the bills paid. *Do you?* If he is wealthy, she will have a high standard of living, along with all his worldly goods being left to her in his will, as well as a trust fund for the kids. *(Do you even have a "tryst fund," mistress?)*

✎ **NOTE:** It is usually the higher echelon of society wives who stay when their husbands cheat, as they have way too much to lose if they leave him. Fat wives also stay, as they know it's doubtful they could ever get anyone else, so they will suffer his crap rather than be alone. *Sad!*

You might be reading this and thinking to yourself, "How can she be saying these things? How can she be so mercenary and so hard?" That means you are still in denial—it might be better if you put this book down now and came back to it when you have experienced a few more lies from your MM. (Trust me, you'll wonder what took you so long to wake up. I did!)

✎ **NOTE:** By the way, sisters, I'm not suggesting you should act like this if you're in an open and honest relationship or that you should treat men like this in general. No. Only under *these* circumstances, with MMs who think they can have it all for nothing, even although they know their situation makes the scales very unfairly tipped in the mistress's favor to begin with!

If you end up exposing your MM as a serial liar (by calling his wife and thus finding out that there was never any spare room stuff going on and that things at home were "good"), you will have a number of emotions to deal with. If you had a good relationship with your MM, you may end up getting over the whole hate thing, and could even continue to see him (if he still dares to carry on with you).

But if you feel that your MM has *totally* misled you and blatantly wasted a certain period of your life, you should get even with him so that he doesn't get away with it!

One very angry mistress I interviewed in London told me how she got even with her MM when he finally conceded that he wasn't going to leave his wife like he'd originally planned to.

They'd been having an intense affair for almost two years, and despite the fact that the angry mistress had called his wife at home one night and told her ALL the juicy details of her husband's affair, he amazingly came back to that same mistress later on!

And can you believe that even although the wife was told *firsthand* just what a liar her husband was, and how he'd been deceiving her for such a length of time, the mousewife stayed with him *(ka-ching!)* and even took the trouble to call up the mistress, who was even angrier by then, to tell her that her hubby had admitted his mistake in having the affair, and that on reflection he was actually "happy" with the way things were and wanted to stay with her and the kids after all. She told the mistress that they were both going to try to make things work between them and that—*get this*—he would be financially compensating her for his misdemeanors (and for all the business class tickets he had bought for his "other woman"). Sounds like there was lot of love going on there—*I don't think!*

Well, his idea of making things work was—after a short time had elapsed—to call the "dismissed mistress" and rekindle the affair with her, even after she had destroyed him by calling his wife and telling her the saucy, in-depth details about him and their affair that would have crushed any normal woman.

He financially compensated the mistress too, no doubt to try and buy her loyalty in the hope that she wouldn't call his wife again. *(It didn't work!)*

The second time around, things got a little fraught between the MM and his still-simmering mistress, especially as he was under constant surveillance by the wife, who believed that they were "making things work as a couple." So after a few months, the affair ended acrimoniously, and yes, you know what's coming. She called the mousewife *again* to advise her that her wayward husband had in fact gone back to his old ways—and his old mistress.

You'd think that after his wife found out a second time, she'd feel foolish for believing him and giving him the chance she did. But nope—she proceeded to stay with him even after the repeat performance! Quite remarkable, huh? As usual, though, because he was worth millions, she put up with it.

This just proves that once a cheater, always a cheater! He had professed to want to work things out with his wife and probably *begged* her not to throw him out, and then he proceeded to get his affair going again. What a shit! (Although a man will never *really* respect a wife who takes him back after his affair is exposed. Would you?)

RECAP NOTES TO MISTRESSES:

- Start as you mean to go on. Set the standards in the beginning; let him know that you expect to be spoiled and cared for, to the best of his ability, as part of the relationship you are both entering into.
- His wife treats their marriage as a business relationship, so you should do the same!
- Be "cute" about your criteria, as no man likes to feel that you are trying to extort him *(even if you are).*
- If you really do care for him, make sure he knows that things could be so much better, easier, and more honest if he just *left his wife.* Always remind him of this when you're trying to barter your lifestyle. It's a really good balance and will help to absolve you from being seen as a gold digger in his eyes.
- If you aren't sure of his intentions and require a test, create a situation where you "need" some financial help. See if he steps up to the table or runs away.
- Ladies, get what you can and enjoy it all without a moment's guilt, as it will never even come close to what the wife is getting from him, nor the pain you may eventually experience if things get heavy.
- Always remember that whatever he expends to keep his two relationships going, he will be spending far more on the wife and kids than on you!

- So, to sum up: *Make yourself important.* Because if you don't, nobody else will!

✎ **FINAL NOTE TO MISTRESSES:** In case you waiver or soften, remember the plain fact in all of this is that he loves his wife more than you, in spite of what he tells you. If that were not the case, he would be with you and not her!

AN EXTRA NOTE TO SUM UP THIS IMPORTANT CHAPTER:

- Wives stay with wayward husbands for financial and lifestyle equilibrium ("for richer or poorer"…just so long as it's not poorer). Wives don't *do* poverty, and they hardly ever "stay" because of feelings; they stay because of the kids. It's a situation that suits both of them and in which they tick along quite nicely. (Don't ever kid yourself on that score.)
- The way an MM views his wife can be best summed up with a car analogy. An MM might fancy a change from the boring, old reliable family car and would enjoy a flashy new ride for a while (i.e., his mistress). But at the end of the day, when it comes down to it, he's comfortable and familiar with the one he's had for the last twenty years. He knows how to get her started when she's cold, plus she's fairly cheap to run and he knows her full service history.

  So he will revel in the temporary thrill of being in something flashy for a change, something that catches everyone's attention and boosts his ego, relieving his boredom (and taking care of any midlife crisis he may be having). And because he knows that he has options now, and *can* get his hands on a "better model," he is more content and quite happy to come back to the one that has been so good to him over the years. Okay, so her suspension might not be great, but she would have to *completely* break down before he bit the bullet and got rid of her, or committed to that new model he uses on a temporary basis, when it suits him. Does that make things a bit clearer, ladies? *(Crystal, I'd say!)*

Mistresses are the real pawns in the affair game, and the ones with the emotions to be played upon. The ones who get reeled in and who become the losers in the end. Because more often than not, they tend to believe that their MMs really *do* want to own that new car, not just ride around in it on the weekends. With that in mind, if you are a mistress, make sure you think about what YOU need. I urge you to look after Number One in all of this, as the other two people "driving" this affair are without question doing what's best for them. And that, my dear sisters, is a fact!

chapter 8

"Can You Talk?"

The Art of Good Communication with Your MM

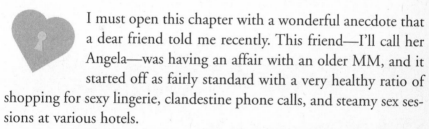 I must open this chapter with a wonderful anecdote that a dear friend told me recently. This friend—I'll call her Angela—was having an affair with an older MM, and it started off as fairly standard with a very healthy ratio of shopping for sexy lingerie, clandestine phone calls, and steamy sex sessions at various hotels.

She quite liked him, and the affair, for what it was. It facilitated a certain type of lifestyle for her, and she enjoyed some okay sex with him too. And although she didn't see him often—which suited her perfectly, as he was retired, seriously wealthy, and always traveling to some exotic place—they made sure to have plenty of steamy phone conversations between meet-ups.

Then suddenly, after one Caribbean trip too many (with his wife), the sun and the sangria must have affected his head, as he started playing hard to get with Angela. He seemingly began to enjoy rubbing her nose in the fact that he had a "blessed life," whilst she was doing her utmost to try and juggle everything single-handedly in order make ends meet for herself and her two teenaged kids!

Anyway, long story short, she *didn't* give up on him (mainly because he was rich), and eventually he came back into play, offering to pay off her huge credit card bills to make up for his "distancing her."

Being a sensible (albeit gorgeous) single mother and grateful for any semblance of help, she jumped at his generosity and they continued with their affair. As time went on, he became rather paranoid about their communication, and although he never articulated that he wanted to stop seeing her, he did expend a lot of brainpower on coming up with a special code that he wanted them to communicate with. (*The Da Vinci Code* had nothing on this guy.)

I have to say, when she first told me the story, my initial reaction was, "Well, it would've been better if he'd put *that much* effort into his relationship with his relatively new wife rather than making secret communication codes with you, *his mistress.*" However, I listened to the story with interest and found that he was taking the subject very seriously indeed and that his code was quite detailed.

Basically, Angela's MM was scared that she might call him on his mobile one day when his wife happened to be alongside him. Even worse, it might happen at a time when she was in the car with him, and his phone was on the hands-free speaker system. If he was making and taking business calls while driving, it meant he might pick up Angela's call by mistake, and his wife would be privy to their conversation (or at least privy to watching him try and squirm out of it). So this is what he came up with to alleviate his concerns.

"Angela, my dear," he said (he was extremely patronizing). "From now on, when you call me, you *must* say you're calling from my lawyer's office." He gave her the name of his lawyer's firm just in case she ever needed to refer to it as part of her script. (It was a triple-barreled name and not the easiest to remember. Let's call it Liar, Cheater, and Bastard Ltd. for argument's sake.)

The MM continued on lucidly: "And then, *my dear*, you must say that you are just calling to see if I have received the fax you sent me earlier.

"Now, if I start to talk about *the fax,*" he went on, "it means my wife is next to me in the car. If that's the case, please act very professionally, dear, and just go along with what I say. Then I'll try to call you back later when I'm alone.

"Obviously, if I talk normally with you, then you know it's safe and we're clear to talk. And you *can* talk dirty to me, my dear." *Chortle, chortle.*

He continued, "I hope you're okay with all of this, Angie, as I just worry that you might call me up one time and innocently say, 'Hello, darling. How are you, my gorgeous?'—which I do love, by the way, don't get me wrong—exactly when *she* is sitting next to me. It would ruin everything, and I would have a lot of explaining to do!"

So Angela, being such a *good* mistress (and more to the point, looking forward immensely to having her credit card bills paid off), went along with it all even though she found the whole thing pathetically nauseating.

Unfortunately though, her MM had forgotten to tell Angie how to act if his wife happened to answer his mobile phone. (God, why are men so stupid and trusting *and stupid?!*)

Angela had her spiel all ready to go on the day of her very first coded call to her MM. So she was more than a little floored (to say the least!) when his wife answered his phone and equally taken aback when she asked her to identify the name of the lawyer's office from which she was calling.

Poor Angie hadn't expected to go as far as ever having to use the name of the law firm when speaking with her MM about "the fax." And being at the wrong end of forty and the first to admit that she's very forgetful with details, she really had to pull it out of the bag—and quickly!

Luckily, the name came back to her, and she got it right enough for the wife to believe her, saying she would pass the message to her husband when he finished his daily tennis lesson out on his private court.

"HAVING AN *Affair?*"

✎ **NOTE TO ALL MISTRESSES:** This is a good example of just how damned lucky MMs are when their mistress covers for them so well…and in some cases so often! Those few minutes of interacting with the wife undoubtedly caused some level of stress to Angie, the mistress. And ironically, while Angie was covering her MM's backside, he was obliviously perfecting his backhand! This case in point proves that mistresses will go along with it all—*until they don't!*

✎ **NOTE TO MARRIED MEN:** And when they *don't*, then little conversations like the above could take a very different route.

✎ **MORAL OF THIS STORY FOR MISTRESSES:** Don't let the facts get in the way of a "good fax"…or land you in a state of flux!

Angela had an even better story when describing how another serious, long-term MM communicated with his wife in front of her sometimes. This was an MM she had been with for six years and with whom she was hopelessly in love, even though she knew she shouldn't be.

She said he would often stand at the end of her bed (while they were in the middle of having sex) to answer a call from his wife, extremely angry that she was phoning at such an inopportune moment, shouting at her, "What the hell do you want? I'm in the middle of an important meeting!"

For men who partake in extramarital affairs, the mobile phone must have truly been a godsend. Apart from the flexibility of being able to say that they are in a *totally* different location or situation than they actually are, there is a whole plethora of new excuses and lies that can be added to their already burgeoning list. Things such as, "My battery was low," "There was no signal," "I was on the subway." Or at the very top of the list: "My mobile was off because I was in a meeting." (LOVE that one!)

Ringing any bells, wives? Is this raising any questions or doubt in your mind when you think back to the numerous occasions when you can't get hold of your husband?

Ringing any bells, mistresses? When you think back to the numerous occasions when *you* can't get hold of her husband?

For mistresses, the "art of communication" with your MM will be prevalent throughout the entire affair, both in quality and longevity. The mobile phone will become your best friend. It is the key to arranging your secret trysts, keeping in touch, sending and receiving messages of desire, and the most important one, of course—*phone sex*. If you're in a long-distance relationship, or if one or the other of you travels a lot, the phone will be even more important in your life. (How on earth did we ever live without mobile phones?)

There is also the wonderful invention of SMS messaging (short message service), more commonly known as text messaging, which is put to *such* good use in the realms of having an affair.

✿ **TIP FOR RED-HOT MISTRESSES:** Sending an explicit text message about what you want to do to your MM when you see him will make him hot under the collar and keep him hot for you, especially if you can time the sending of your message to coincide with when he is, say, just going into a stuffy board meeting or just boarding a long flight. You will drive him wild and keep him coming back for more. Text messages are cheap, easy to send, and a huge investment in the world of illicit communications.

Also, as Angela advised me in our interview, some phones have the ability to make and send two-minute videos, which are transmitted in a similar way as a text message, but will provide a private little porn show. Apparently Angie teased her MM on many a late-night occasion with such things. In the end, he actually used to beg her to "please send a video" most nights they were apart. Needless to say, she soon got bored when it was expected of her. In the end, she decided to stop with the videos altogether, leaving her MM beside himself!

Finally, there are also the palm-held BlackBerry or Treo devices, which mean you can enjoy regular e-mailing with your MM, anytime, anywhere.

✎ **NOTE TO MISTRESSES:** E-mailing is *so* much cheaper than sending text messages, but not always as accessible.

If your MM has as good a grasp of his technical equipment as he does his *own* equipment, then he can receive your e-mails via his mobile phone and reply either as a text message or as an e-mail without needing to physically go to his computer. This eliminates his wife being alerted to any unusual cyber activity in the process.

The creation of mobile telephones should make it very easy for you to get in touch with your MM (although awkward at the same time if he is with the Mrs., not to mention if she ever saw all those dirty text messages you send him and the huge number of calls he makes to you).

I heard a funny story from a friend of mine who met a man a while ago, who was well known for his association with the British royal family. (She actually met him at Prince Charles and Camilla's wedding, and he asked for her number over some light small talk at the finger buffet.)

They had a number of phone conversations, and although they tried, they never actually got to meet up for "a drink." Although he had insisted on trying to as soon as possible because he thought she was sooo sexy. In fact, he was all over her like a telephonic rash!

He wasn't married, but he did have a long-term partner named Maureen who obviously thought they were an item (enough to check up on him, anyway). Maureen was looking for answers to some suspicions she had, and one night she sent a suggestive text to my friend, from her partner's phone, pretending she was the man in question. My friend, seeing a text from this man's number, bit the bait and text-messaged him back immediately, pleased to have heard from him again. A couple of nanoseconds later, she received a call from "long-term Maureen," about to tear her off a strip for sniffing around her man. Something in his behavior must have alerted Maureen, and she was secretly going through all of the women's numbers in his phone, sending them text messages as a test, reeling them in to see what sort of tone the replies would bring.

Unfortunately, all Maureen went away with were some long-lasting comments from my friend and some hard truths about the man she was trying to set the stupid honey trap to catch!

✎ **NOTE TO SISTERS WITH A SENSE OF HUMOR:** The soooo sexy woman in question was Angie, *again,* and we still laugh about it to this day.

Hopefully for the MM's sake, his mobile telephone will be a company phone not a private one, meaning the bills will go to his office, not to his house—and not to his wife's eyes.

An MM will never use his mistress's real name when saving her number in his phone. She will be saved in his contact list under a pseudonym, a male name, or perhaps under the auspice of his local mechanic.

✎ **"INSIDER" NOTE TO WIVES:** Your husband may be saving his mistress's number as a man's name so that if he is in the shower, let's say, and you happen to see a text or a call coming in on his phone from Dave, John, or Simon, you won't think twice about it. As opposed to seeing the same coming from Diana, Joanne, or Stephanie, when you *might* be more "alerted." You could mess up his whole day if you answered it. (You gotta love him for being so smart!)

It is to simplify matters that most MMs tend to choose a male name for their mistress, which either begins with the same letter as her real name, or one that sounds phonetically similar to the female version.

✎ **NOTE TO MISTRESSES:** If he has more than one mistress, then this "filing" system will be essential for him to implement, in order to remember you all and not get you mixed up. I once knew of an MM who stored his mistresses' names backward, so *Sarah*, for example, would be *Haras*.

When the cheating MM is with his wife, if he has any sense, he will just switch his phone off altogether. Although this will probably infuriate you, because then you will *know* that he's at home with his wife!

✎ **NOTE TO MISTRESSES:** You will probably come to obsess over this "home time," so try to watch out for that.

If he happens to be technically savvy, he may put his mobile on vibrate or silent ring when he's at home, which means he can monitor his calls and nobody but him (and his inside trouser pocket) knows who's calling. In this case, if he sees your number and his wife isn't near him, he'll take your call. If she is near him, he'll let it go to voice mail (and you'll realize that). It could be even worse if he answers and talks to you in stilted conversation. Wouldn't that drive you mad, too?

All in all, vibration seems to be a better option than being switched off, for all concerned.

Text messaging is a good way of keeping in touch when he's at home. But if your MM isn't a regular texter, this could send signs to his wife that he's texting with a woman (or at least it should if she pays attention to such things).

Let's look a little closer at the subject of text messaging. There are the "late-night texters," usually an MM whose wife has gone to bed before him, allowing him the space to text his mistress (especially as he will be feeling horny so late at night). It will be your choice whether you indulge him by answering his pleas for attention at this late hour.

🗝 **ADVICE TO MISTRESSES:** Don't allow yourself to be available just to suit his needs like this, especially if you don't think you're getting what you want out of the affair (or if you need to wake up early for work the next day). Never feel sorry for him! Always remember that he has a wife upstairs, and if he was *nicer* to her, *she* might be more inclined to "help him out."

Typically, a late-night text messaging MM would undoubtedly also relish one of those little video messages of you doing something very provocative. Again, your choice, mistresses. It is definitely a powerful way of reeling him in at the beginning, but will no doubt grate on your patience as he becomes reliant on such things.

✎ **NOTE TO MISTRESSES:** Late-night texting and videoing with your MM, especially when he's at home, will give you a feeling of being in control in a sort of "imagine if his wife only knew what he was doing with me" kind of way.

Let us bear in mind that there are many different types of MM when it comes to communications with a mistress. There are those who don't give a rat's ass about the wife and who *totally* wear the trousers at home. This type will usually answer his phone at any time at all and act completely un-phased. He may pretend you're a male buddy with the offer to call you back in a while, or perhaps make out that you are his personal assistant or a business associate requesting to send him a fax or something. (Alternatively he may just take the call and talk normally to you because he doesn't *care* what she thinks and he hates her anyway.)

The type of MMs who are *really* scared of getting found out (usually the same ones who *don't* have an unbearable marriage) will definitely switch off their phone when they are at home so as to immerse themselves into their "other life." Therefore, you should know from the beginning that if you ever need to get hold of your MM, let's say in an emergency (or even just because you miss him and want to talk), you can forget it until the next day when he checks his messages. At that time, you will probably rant and rave about how upset you were that you couldn't get in touch with him, and a series of arguments and accusations will boringly ensue.

✎ **NOTE TO MISTRESSES:** This will bring home to you the fact that he is definitely *not* your boyfriend, as I tried to tell you earlier, but that he is in fact somebody else's husband (and perhaps meal ticket), with whom you just happen to be having sex…period!

Your MM will proceed to lie about why he didn't get back to you sooner. (You could be stretched out in hospital for all he knows!) But in truth, it was just as I said—the phone was switched off because he was having a nice family time at home and, perhaps, entertaining family friends (blah, blah).

An MM once told me, when I couldn't get him for more than a day, that his mobile was switched off because he had taken the kids to the zoo, claiming it was the first outing he'd ever taken them on without their mother, and that I would've been so proud of him! He tried to tell me, when I questioned how he could shut down for twenty-four hours, that his business life had been put on hold too, claiming that even his secretary hadn't been able to contact him while he'd been busy feeding the monkeys. (Yeah, right! He must have felt at home, as he turned out to be the biggest monkey of them all. *Pass me the peanuts!*)

Meanwhile, Angie discovered the hard way about not being able to reach her long-term MM when he was *en famille.* She had been out to dinner with him on a Friday night and had used her credit card (although *why* I don't know). Anyhow, she realized the next day that she had lost her card, so she urgently needed to speak with her MM to ask him to go back to the restaurant, which was near where he lived, to see if she'd left it there.

Alas, it was the weekend, so by the time he switched on his phone again and returned her calls, it was Monday morning on his way to work—too late! She had cancelled her card and also went on to cancel him out of her life. She was so irate at not being able to get in touch with him when she needed him, it proved to her what she needed to know. Losing her card taught her the lesson that she needed to lose the man too!

Mistresses, an MM will have a list of excuses for you about why he can't easily receive calls at home—things such as his mobile phone doesn't work in his house, or it does, but only ever so slightly and only in certain places. Or because the reception is so bad, there's only one area where it works, and if he moves an inch off that spot, *boom,* it's gone. (Ha! I used to believe *that* one.)

🕻 **NOTE TO CYNICAL MISTRESSES:** I'll bet, sure as hell, that the reception is perfect when they call from all corners of their house to instigate late-night phone sex with you.

Okay, so now we've looked at some of the background behind the art of good communication with your MM. Now let's look at some of the interaction skills a good mistress should possess, and those three little words that should roll off her tongue each time she calls him up. (No, silly. Not "I love you." *Are you crazy?*)

"Can You Talk?"
The Art of Good Communication with Your MM

When you call your MM and he answers, *whatever* time of the day or night it might be, and wherever you think he is or isn't, you should always ask, "Can you talk?" Then follow his lead. He will love you for this, because if he really *cannot* talk (whether it's due to him being at home or truly in a meeting at work), you are giving him the option and not just blatantly launching into a conversation with him. If he can't talk and you don't check with him first, he will inevitably have to hang up on you or, alternatively, keep repeating "Hello? Hello?" into his phone, feigning poor reception on his end. Both instances will infuriate you (dangerous!), so for damage limitation purposes all round, always ask the question. Show him you care by using *those* three important little words. There is nothing worse for an MM than being in a position of awkwardness, with his mistress yabbering on at the other end.

✎ **NOTE TO MISTRESSES:** He could *really* be in that business meeting he told you about or with his boss or a client. And remember, mistresses, you need to ultimately support him in his work duties so that he is able to earn that extra money to support *you*, and his affair with you. (A good "note to self" would be to try and cut him a bit of slack now and again when it comes to things like this.)

Now, the tone of voice you use when calling him is very important too. The MM always wants to make sure that the affair is as easy and enjoyable *for him* as possible, as a reminder of just why he is risking "so much" to be with you. So if you can always try to have a happy voice and an upbeat attitude, you will go far with him.

The key thing to remember is that you should always appear to be "different" from his wife—not a moaner or a nag (notice I left out *groaner*, as you have *carte blanche* to be one of those in the bedroom). And not talking about mundane, boring practical matters nor obligating him to specific dates and times (like parent-teacher meetings, for example), as all this could lead him to feeling under pressure!

✐ **TIP FOR MISTRESSES:** You can and should, of course, not hold back on pressuring him regarding any and all dates and obligations that he has with you, pinning him down to timings and venues as much as necessary. Just be careful to do it in such a way that he doesn't realize what you're doing, but that gives you the result you want in the end.

Basically, make it a joy for him to call you (even if you may not feel very joyous at times). As we have established, it's all a game and if you let your true emotions show and become inflexible or difficult to deal with (or, God forbid, *pushy and manipulative),* he will drop you like a used condom because he'll be wary of the way the relationship is headed and won't want to deal with the drama.

On the subject of communication, the more you fall for him, the more inclined you'll be to hang on his every call, and the *promise* of his calls. Often, for a time, you may even start to believe the lies he's feeding you about why he doesn't call. (That period will hopefully blow over, and you will be back on top of his lies again soon enough.)

Always remember you aren't dealing with a regular person here—you're dealing with an MM—a cheater and a fraud. If you ever think of him or refer to him as a "boyfriend," you are going to be sadly let down, so don't do it. *Know that from the start!*

He has to earn the title of boyfriend, and he *certainly* isn't going to do that by keeping his wife in the frame (in other words, keeping his options open). Don't sell yourself short. You have options too, so make him work hard for you—*you are worth it!*

And by working hard, I mean, for example, don't *always* be available to take his calls (even if you are). Keep him on his toes, and let him occasionally wonder where you are and *with whom.* Whilst he is living out his boring, mundane suburban life with his wife, having their boring couples dinners down at the local restaurant, it will kill him to think of you out with another man or perhaps dancing the night away at some fancy club full of beautiful people. (Even if you need to lie and tell him you're out tripping the light fantastic but are really sitting at home watching TV, he won't ever know!)

Use this scenario to your advantage. It's your trump card, and don't worry about the lying part—it will become dead easy for you as you learn and perfect the art from *him*, proving that he did in fact teach you something valuable along the way.

A friend of mine recently made a wonderful personal discovery with regards to keeping track of her MM (without him knowing it), when she realized that upon sending a text message from her phone, she could have a delivery report sent back to her when the person *actually* opened it. This report was delivered to the sender only when the recipient had literally opened and read the text, which means his mobile had to be switched on in the first place!

They were going through the motions of breaking up, and he foolishly was trying to ignore her, thinking she would go away quietly. She, meanwhile, was calling his mobile nonstop and was *beyond* rage that it was continually switched off. When she realized she had this option, she sent him a message, and as soon as she received the delivery report, she immediately rang his number. Often the report was delivered hours or even days later, but she was ready to pounce as soon as she got it.

Even if he didn't take her call the first time, she kept ringing him repeatedly (being sure to withhold her number, of course) until he had to answer. He had to use his phone, or he would never have been able to collect his *other* text messages and voice mails. Plus, by her blocking her number, he wouldn't actually know who it was and might think he was missing another "important" call. She told me that she had enjoyed administering this form of telephonic abuse immensely.

✎ **NOTE TO MISTRESSES:** Whilst this method was discovered in the face of a breakup, it can be used in times of peace too. For example, you can send your MM a steamy text and follow up on it moments later to reiterate what you'd like to do to him (knowing he has already read the first one). He will think you are "so hot" and "so cool"! And he can never again say that he didn't receive a text message you sent him. It's like your own personal radar system for your MM. (It goes without saying never to tell him about this, of course!)

I think I have covered most topics of communication in this chapter. Your MM is by default a selfish man, or he wouldn't have the capacity to have an affair and make the time for it. I'm sure he wants to talk to you as much as possible—but only when it suits *him*, which is after the corporate meetings, the golf, the tennis, and the wife and the kids. Somewhere on his to-do list, when all the boxes have been checked, he will definitely call you and tell you that you mean *everything* to him. Even though this will probably be around midnight, when he has some down time (and a box of Kleenex!) to himself. *Go figure!*

RECAP NOTES TO MISTRESSES:

- Don't make communication easy for him; you are not there to *help* him have his affair with you.
- Don't always be available to talk—even if you are. In other words, don't let him take you for granted. His perception should be that you are popular, busy, and in demand *even if you're not*. He has to know how lucky he should feel to have you, and he should be made to feel constantly insecure at the thought of losing you to another *available* man, coupled with a few pangs of jealousy now and again about where you are and with whom (when you *don't* answer his calls). Though this will never come even close to the *ping-pang-pongs* of jealousy that a mistress will feel toward her MM and his wife when *they're* together!

✎ **FINAL TIP OF ADVICE TO MISTRESSES:** I can't emphasize the last point, about keeping him on his adulterous toes, strongly enough, ladies. *Really play on it.* If he wants you to be more available to him, he might need to spoil you more, to make you feel special enough to *want* to hang around waiting for him while he spends his life with another woman! Do I finally hear a *ka-ching* in your favor, ladies?

chapter 9

"If Only I'd Met You Years Ago..."

And Other Bullshit Lines

 This is a great one, although it won't take long to explain. A typical trait of an MM who partakes in having an extramarital affair (especially a well-weathered MM) is to neither face up to, nor deal with, the reality and enormity of the precarious situation he has created. He will typically bury his head in the sand. An MM having an affair absolutely *dreads* looking into the future and having to deal with the reality of the two different lives he is promising his two different women.

✎ **NOTE TO MMs:** The only thing you get by digging your head in the sand is sand in your hair!

Therefore, when an unhappily married man has fallen heavily for his mistress, why wouldn't he think something like, "Wow, I've finally met the woman of my dreams. How can I change things with regards to my situation so that the two of us can have the best possible chance of a life together? I'm such a lucky guy, and I certainly don't want to risk losing her by not leaving my wife, so I will try to do whatever it takes to make things work in our favor."

✓ **REALITY CHECK:** *No way!* That is NOT how he will think at all.

"HAVING AN ♥ *Affair?*"

For the adulterous MM, it is far simpler to be in denial. (This is the first step to starting any affair anyway.) As a result, it's easier for him to say, *"If only* I had met you years ago." This is a safe way for him to express how he feels about you, instead of having the balls to find a realistic way of being with you in the here and now. At the same time, it won't give you those "ideas above your station" I mentioned earlier. It's a sort of backhanded compliment, if you will.

✎ **NOTE TO MISTRESSES:** This statement might make an impression on you when you first hear it fall from his lips, as it can be quite touching if delivered in the right way. However, in reality, it is a totally futile and inane statement and, quite frankly, a waste of his breath. It comes under the category of "should've, could've, would've...but *didn't!"*

When you hear the "I wish I'd met you years ago," line for the first time, you might be really flattered, but try to see past it, especially if you notice that nothing else he says is very forthcoming either.

✎ **NOTE TO MISTRESSES:** Make a mental note of the number of years ago your MM tells you he *wished* he'd met you.

For example, if he has been married ten years, note whether he says he wishes he had met you ten years ago *(before* he got married, thus implying that he wishes he could be married to you instead). If he has been married for ten years but wishes he'd met you eight years ago, that means he was happy for two of them and so on and so forth. *(You'll work it out if you're smart.)*

✎ **NOTE TO MISTRESSES:** If this grown man is going to bandy around such information to you willy-nilly, then don't you think he at least needs to be held accountable to it? As we know, men, *especially* MMs, hate to be held accountable for anything, especially something they have said.

Now, the ages of the MM's kids can often be a telltale benchmark behind this statement he makes to a mistress. A friend of mine's was easy—he told her that he wished he had met her four years ago. He had twin boys that were four years old, so that was an easy figure for him to come up with. Even though at the time (in her love cocktail stage), she couldn't help being niggled that he hadn't said *five* years ago, as that would have covered the conception and incubation period of his kids too. But, hey, they're just minor details, and as we know, men don't "do details"—major *or* minor. (What great names for twins — Major and Minor!)

If your MM has kids of different ages, let's say fifteen and ten, I doubt he'll say, "I wish I'd met you fifteen years ago" (thus hitting on the oldest kid in his marriage). He will no doubt revert to the original generic line of "If only I'd met you years ago" as a more general and polite statement.

Now, mistresses, if you're on the receiving end of this line and you're "in love" with your MM, you could find yourself being temporarily brainwashed into daydreaming about the fact that you too wish you had met him before he committed to *her*, wishing you could change your past. (Anything... just so *you* can be with him, right?)

✎ **NOTE TO SELF:** I did, mentally reverting through my life, trying to go back in time to see if there would have been *any way* to reconstruct it, to see if we would've ever met. How sick is that! Even more worrying was the amount of time I allowed the whole fantasy of "what ifs" to play out in my mind when I could've been doing something far more productive instead.

If your MM also happens to be feeding you the line that he wants to "find a way" to leave his wife for you, in tandem with "I wish I'd met you years ago," you may naturally think he's about to make some changes!

✎ **NOTE TO MISTRESSES:** If you're ever lucky enough to have his wife suspect him and confront him over whether he's having an affair, he should (if he *ever* meant any of what he told you about wanting to leave her) seize that as an ideal opportunity to come clean with her and get out of his situation.

Sadly, most MMs take the path of least resistance when cornered. They do anything to wheedle their way back into the wife's good books (until enough dust has settled for them to go out and cheat again).

Frighteningly, men tend to wheedle very well. I heard a shocking statistic that ninety-five percent of wives who had taken part in a survey and hired a private investigator to follow their philandering husbands actually stayed and worked at the marriage even when their husbands had been caught red-handed cheating on them. This is a scary concept—and very embarrassing for the rest of the self-respecting female gender.

Based on this information, mistresses, I'm sorry to say that you haven't got a hope in hell of him ever leaving his wife for you—*even if she does find out!*

✎ **NOTE:** As an MM once told me, "I *will* leave my wife, but it has to be on my terms, when *I'm* ready." Such big words, backed up with such little action—a true case study of what I was saying earlier. Because when his wife did find out about his affair (in complete detail), he still stayed and she still kept him. *Sigh…*

Here's a thought for all you mistresses: Even if your MM, "his holiness" of the marital world, ever did deem to leave his wife, when *he* was ready (though in reality, it's more like when his wife came to her senses and couldn't take anymore, or met someone else herself and threw him out), it could be way too late for you. The little weasel may have shown you his palette of true colors once too often, leaving you washed out and ready to start a new slate without him!

If his wife really did throw him out, it's a far less attractive scenario than if he had left her and came to you of his own volition. An affair might become slightly *less* exciting when the MM in question is suddenly available 24/7, dirty socks and all!

RECAP NOTES TO MISTRESSES:

- Try not to allow yourself to live in *his* fantasy world of "wishing and hoping," and generally just enjoying *only* the present situation (your affair) without considering the future (even if you only consider it privately to yourself). At least have some personal plans and some (of his) savings put by, in case he tries to leave you high and dry.
- He will fight you on this "planning for the future" bit due to head-in-sand syndrome, but stick to your guns. He will only fight you on it because he wants to continue having you *and* his wife in his life. He wants to continue to have it all for as long as he can. Remember, mistresses, as I always tell you, you are not the ones *having it all* (or nowhere near enough, anyway).
- As with everything else he tells you, be aware of the "I wish I'd met you years ago" statement. If he really means it, he'll act upon it and make up for the time he has allegedly lost. (Don't hold your breath on this one!)

chapter 10

"I'm Not Sleeping with My Wife"

And More Lies

 Okay, this is a *great* subject. Your MM will often tell you from the outset that he does not sleep with his wife and that he hasn't "for years." Sometimes an MM will tell you that they don't even sleep in the same bed, and that he has his own room and she has hers...BLAH, BLAH, BLAH. Athough it is far more likely he will tell you that they do sleep in the same bed, but there is little or no physical relationship between them, and that they hardly ever "do anything" unless—and I quote an MM here—"I *have* to perform." (Told you they're great actors!)

The same clown of an MM went on to qualify his actions to me, telling me that if on occasion he had to perform, "It only lasts five minutes, and it's a total nightmare." Which left me wondering which was worse—knowing that he actually did have sex with his Mrs. or reveling in the fact that he thought it was a nightmare! In truth, the one sort of balanced out the other, although his version of it being a nightmare was debatable, I'm sure. But at least it saved him the trouble of masturbating and that meant his wife came in useful for a change.

✎ **REALITY NOTE TO ALL MISTRESSES:** At least 99.9 percent of the time, there is *never* a "spare room scenario." He will be sharing the same marital bed with his wife that he always has, and will do so until death or disaster do them part, so never believe otherwise! Whether they actually *do* anything is a whole other story, one you will never know the real facts about.

Your MM may actually be telling the truth about *not* having sex with his wife. Rule of thumb is that it is pretty obvious there must be some trouble between the sheets. Otherwise why would he have come sniffing around *your* comforter in the first place?

This is compounded by the very fact that many wives—if they're angry or upset with their husbands (so that's most of them)—take away the sex as a form of punishment (although some MMs I've spoken to might see it as a relief). It is only "re-earned" when he has "righted his wrongs." Sometimes the poor chap can never "re-earn" it, so this embargo can go on for months—*years* in many cases. Sometimes too much time elapses for sanctions ever to be lifted successfully again. This results in a very horny, frustrated husband, and thus it can be argued that some wives help bring his affair on themselves.

✎ **NOTE TO WIVES:** Your course of "punishment" really *doesn't* work. It just gives your husband the excuse he needs in order to validate having a mistress (or to find himself one pronto if he doesn't already have one on standby). If and when you do find out about his affair, and you both end up talking your problems through (i.e., the reasons why he strayed), this will be the first thing he throws at you when he backpedals to try and save his marriage. (Just trying to be helpful here, wives—trying to keep you in the loop and all that good stuff.)

Some while into your affair, he may also tell you that he can't even make love to his wife these days because all he sees *your* face. Now, you may well be flattered by that statement in the beginning, but as with the "I wish I'd met you years ago" line, do *not* be fooled or taken in by it. Because think about it: He actually means that he *can and does* make love to his wife; he just sees your face instead of hers!

✎ **PRAGMATIC NOTE TO SELF:** Oops, slap on wrist—it's just called "sex" or "having to perform" (and is a nightmare task at home…I forgot!). But the bottom line is that whether he's seeing your face or whatever else, he is still able to take care of business and get the job done! (Bastard!)

Actually, the very fact that he's thinking of you will help him to achieve and sustain a better erection, resulting in—yep, you got it—the wife ultimately getting a better sex session than usual because of your "presence" in his (and their) life. This leads me to wonder who is actually getting shafted the most in the whole triangle of deceit. It also gives weight to my suggestion that a mistress is actually a benevolent marriage counselor, one who is now doubling up as a "soft porn sexual aid" too!

☛ **HARSH AND MERCENARY NOTE TO MISTRESSES:** Do you see what I mean about you *not* being the one who is having it all in the affair, and how the wife is always benefiting from things more than you? (And let's face it—he sure as hell isn't thinking of *her* when he's doing you!)

Mistresses, at the end of the day, whatever spin your MM tries to use to indoctrinate you into believing that he doesn't want to have to have sex with his wife, the bottom line is that he manages to get hard in order to "perform," so she can't be *that* bad, or he wouldn't even be able to get it up at all!

✎ **REITERATION NOTE TO SELF:** *Bastards!*

For a while you may even find yourself thinking, "Oh well, I guess he has to do it; he has to keep his marriage going for the sake of his kids."

☛ **LOUD NOTE OF PLEA:** Please, mistresses, don't *ever* think along those lines, as that would just make his life *complete* if you got into that frame of mind with him.

There are no compromises, allowances, or reasons that can ever make it okay for him to have you both, even though he will try to validate it over and over again to you. Never get into the mindset where you accept "it"—him having sex with his wife—because you will definitely be creating a rod for your own back if you do. You can *know* that he does it, or deal with it for what it is, but please never think of it as okay or, even worse, support him in *any way* with regards to "it"!

✎ **NOTE TO MISTRESSES (those who don't care about "it"):** If you are a mistress who is not in love with your MM (not enough to be bothered that he is sleeping with his wife, anyway), it probably means you're just using him and/or your affair for something to your advantage and that you are in control, which as you know, I am all for. *Use him and lose him, girlfriend!*

But if that is the case, and you do have your own agenda, I would advise you to at least *pretend* to seem a little bothered about this subject matter. Pretending to be a little jealous about him sleeping with his wife could actually do you some good in the long run and stand you in prime stead for some extra "guilt gifts" and "making-up trophies" that all good mistresses know and love (and quite rightly come to expect). This way, as you endeavor to keep your emotions detached, you will also be milking the system at the same time. Well done, girls, I'm proud of you!

✎ **NOTE TO MISTRESSES (those who do care):** If you choose to buy into and *accept* the fact that the man you love is sleeping with another woman, you are nuts and it will drive you loco if you surrender to the hurt, jealousy, and total despair that will accompany your "acceptance." *(Don't say I didn't warn you!)*

If you're in love with your MM, you will realize during your affair that the nights apart will become very long (when he is in bed with her), and depending on your personality, you could find yourself obsessing over it.

✎ **NOTE TO READERS:** I know I said never to let yourself fall in love with an unavailable man, but in this chapter—due to its sensitive content—I have to reach out to those mistresses who *have* fallen in love with their MMs, because I know you are out there, and I too have been in your position. Sometimes you can't stop it happening until it's too late; we are only human after all. And when you're in it, you are in it *deep*. The very nature of the situation and the emotions involved make it very intense, and with such heightened states of mind, one doesn't always think rationally, and things can go either way.

If you aren't in love, then this chapter won't be so pertinent to you, but if you are and you're dealing with the emotional fallout associated with it, I feel it is my duty to reach out to you.

✎ **REMINDER NOTE TO MISTRESSES:** I will be acknowledging the notion of being in love with your MM for this chapter only!

Now, if your MM has told you that he is sleeping in the spare room *(Ha! Big laugh out loud!)*, you'll want to believe it. Really, you will, and why shouldn't you? Why would your MM lie to you, eh? Especially since he has described the spare room in such detail. It must be true. (As I already mentioned in chapter three, we know that men don't usually *do* details…unless it suits them!)

✎ **NOTE:** The first indicator of men lying is that they're not consistent about what they do or don't do. It will be based on whatever suits them at the time to keep all parties happy, which translates to keeping *himself* happy.

So let's recap things so far: Whatever tales your MM might be spinning you, it comes down to the fact that he's doing so in order *not* to have to change his life, but at the same time professing that he wants to, and is trying to, "if only you can bear with him that little bit longer." (Remember, they *are* good actors after all.)

✎ **NOTE:** This is a pretense, him promising you a future together while the reality is that he's putting your present on hold as he keeps you hanging by an invisible umbilical cord.

If you had the misfortune to be reeled in by some of the lies your MM told you in the first place about *not* sleeping with his wife, when you actually learn that your MM has been lying to you (as he is and always was), and moreover that you have allowed him to, there is only one word to sum up how you will feel, and that's *STUPID!*

💣 **NOTE TO "STUPID" MISTRESSES:** There is only one way to deal with things if your MM takes you for a fool and leaves you feeling stupid, and that's *revenge!*

However, sometimes you have to admit to yourself that if you had to do it all again, you might have put yourself in the same situation anyway, because it's true that you do have to follow your heart and at least explore your feelings at the time. We mustn't beat ourselves up for that, as we don't want to be stupid, *and* black and blue!

A liar has to have a great memory to have longevity. And as we are proving so far, we sisters are far sharper than men can ever hope to be—*especially cheating, married ones.* It won't be long before you're bound to catch him out.

Now, back to the spare room scenario. If your affair is becoming increasingly serious and you're becoming increasingly angry that he's still sleeping with his wife (and you are pushing him and pushing him on it), your MM may want to prove to you that he is doing *something* toward trying to change the parameters of his relationship with his wife, working up the nerve to eventually tell her that he is leaving. It is at this point that he may tell you he has moved into the spare room. In his mind, if he convinces you on this one, it'll make everything okay because he will have taken away the thing that bothers you the most (short-term gain, remember). He can, therefore, buy himself more time *not* to tell his wife that he is leaving and more time to carry on his affair with you. He will have placated you, while you foolishly believe that he is taking the small steps required for you and him to be together!

🖊️ **NOTE OF CALCULATION TO MISTRESSES:** If your MM tells you that he sleeps in the spare room, be sure to ask in the beginning (and off the cuff) how many bedrooms are in his house. Let's say he tells you he has four bedrooms, but you know he has three kids—there ain't no spare room for him to be sleeping in even if he wanted to. Go figure! C'mon sisters—wake up!

"I'm Not Sleeping with My Wife"
And More Lies

When you eventually do wise up and start to question if he's sleeping in the spare room (and why are you questioning it, ladies? Is something he's saying just not ringing true?), you will be slapped with even more to think about, and obsess over, than before. Now you will have doubt in your mind regarding the sex issue. (I hate doubt and am personally not comfortable in confusion. In fact, I think that doubt, in many cases, can be worse than knowing the truth.)

I have a true story about an MM who was trying to placate his mistress in this way because she had threatened to end the affair since he was still sleeping with his wife. He called her up a few days after she had told him it was over to say that he had "done it!" He had slept in the spare room for the first night ever. He went on to say how good he felt, and he answered any and all questions from his mistress surrounding this subject. He even said that his wife had been okay with it.

He kept up the pretense for some time, and each time the mistress questioned him about it, he would say, "Oh, it's the norm now. I have my room and she has hers, and the kids run into each of our rooms in the morning." He was so vocal and so believable, even telling the mistress that he fantasized about her and "took care of himself" beneath the sheets in his spare room, which he said turned him on immensely!

✎ **NOTE TO "BELIEVING" MISTRESSES:** His mistress, finally pushed by despair and realizing that she was being taken for a fool, decided to call up his wife a year later and tell her about her wayward husband's affair. The call was very edifying for the mistress, as his wife told her that there had never been a spare room scenario. Not only that, the mistress also learned that her *allegedly* unhappily married lover enjoyed quite a good sex life with his wife, and that generally he "had a ball" when he was at home with her and the kids! His wife was quoted as saying, "I'm shocked because I really thought everything was okay between us."

So, really, what I'm trying to say here is that what you know about—even if the subject is a tough one—you can generally deal with. But the thought of not knowing if he's *really* sleeping in the spare room will eat you up. And how about this one? What if he is sleeping in the spare room like he says? And what if his wife asks him to come back to the marital bed, or indeed goes to him in the night? What would he do? Would he have to "perform"? (Just for the sake of the children, of course.)

✎ **NOTE TO MISTRESSES:** As I have said before, an MM will always have sex with his wife if she instigates it. So whilst he may not start the proceedings himself, he will definitely get the job done if his wife opens the pearly gates.

Mistresses, I'm sure you will have a million thoughts and self-damaging images about how he lives his life at home. And as you roll over in your empty bed to sleep alone, fantasizing and possibly blowing things out of all proportion in absence of the truth, you will feel jealous of his wife (who may or may not be sleeping next to him).

✎ **NOTE:** The more you grow to care about your MM, the more this whole subject will become like mental wrist slashing for you. It's at this point where alcohol will play a huge and valuable role in you actually getting to sleep at all!

The longer you allow these emotions to fester inside you, the more you are on a slippery downward slope *(and well on the road to AA!)*.

✎ **NOTE TO MISTRESSES:** Please try to spot and monitor this behavior. Otherwise your work, health, and looks will suffer very quickly. Rest assured that the wife isn't downing a bottle of wine or gin to help *her* get to sleep at night. She isn't letting the situation get her down or rock her boat, now is she?

Mistresses, you might think that the easiest way to deal with the jealousy is to do the same as he's doing…for instance, being with someone else or dating other people. You can try, but if you think you love your MM, you will find this difficult to carry out.

An MM once said to me, "But if you see other people, it's because you *want to* and you will do lots of fun things with them. That's not fair! I'm not doing any of those things with my wife. We've been together too long, which is part of the problem in the first place!"

A friend of mine was having an affair with a world-famous TV chef, well known on both sides of the Atlantic. He complained to my friend that things weren't going well between him and his wife and that he was being made to sleep in the basement of his mansion.

Enjoying his neediness—and him in general—they spent many a cozy evening together at her tiny (shoddy and cute) apartment in London. Time was always short, and during one particularly hot session, he had to leave by 6 a.m. in order to prepare breakfast at his new restaurant.

Later that day, whilst passing a newsstand, she was flabbergasted to see her MM's face emblazoned all over a top glossy weekly magazine, along with his wife and the latest addition to their growing brood. The article focused on how "strong" their marriage was and just *how much* they loved each other. So much for things not going well at home and him sleeping in the basement...and for him loving his wife *so much* that he was sleeping with another woman a couple times a week. They didn't mention that bit in the celebrity interview! Needless to say, my friend was shocked and felt extremely used and stupid, to say the least.

✎ **GENERAL SUMMARIZATION NOTE TO MISTRESSES:** *Never believe a damned word your MM says!*

chapter 11

Surviving Christmas as a Mistress

And Other Holidays

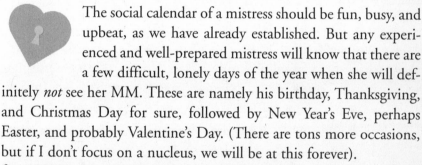 The social calendar of a mistress should be fun, busy, and upbeat, as we have already established. But any experienced and well-prepared mistress will know that there are a few difficult, lonely days of the year when she will definitely *not* see her MM. These are namely his birthday, Thanksgiving, and Christmas Day for sure, followed by New Year's Eve, perhaps Easter, and probably Valentine's Day. (There are tons more occasions, but if I don't focus on a nucleus, we will be at this forever).

✎ **NOTE OF APOLOGY TO MISTRESSES OF ALL RELIGIONS:** I apologize if you feel I'm skipping over things like Passover, Hanukkah, Diwali, and other holidays of different faiths, but I can't cover them all. So, sisters, if you're Jewish, Muslim, Buddhist, or any other religion, perhaps you would indulge me by using Christmas as the main example here and tailor-making the advice to suit your particular needs. Thank you, sisters of the world. I appreciate your solidarity in this matter.

Now, ladies, as we have already ascertained, we know that you have a choice as to whether to be a mistress, but the bottom line is that if you *are* one, then some of the nicest, most joyous occasions of the year will take on a whole different aspect when you spend them alone, and alone you are for all intents and purposes.

Yet it isn't actually as cut-and-dried as that, is it? Because whilst physically, yes, you are alone, in theory you are also one half of an illicit partnership, where the other person is telling you that he wants you and wants to be with you (and is probably doing all the right things to make you fall in love with him—*except* making the right moves required to follow through and be with you).

Therefore, the social celebrations that most people traditionally rejoice in spending together are bound to be tough for you, as they act as a reminder of just what he *isn't* doing. It's not easy for you. Trust me, I know!

I would say that Christmas must be the hardest public holiday to endure in the capacity of being a mistress. It's much harder than just being an SUW at Christmastime. (Thanksgiving is probably on a par, as it is also such a family time.) And because there is so much hype attached to these "magical family times"—when all and sundry are planning their celebrations, shopping, cooking, and wearing of new outfits—you, as a mistress, can't escape it even if you try. It's all around you. Nor can you help but imagine what your MM will be doing with his family while you're home alone.

✎ **NOTE TO MISTRESSES:** You may feel some animosity toward your MM when he is ensconced in "family time" over the Christmas period with his wife and kids (remember what we said about his situation not being that bad or he wouldn't be able to stay in it?). You will find it even harder still if he takes them away on a winter holiday or skiing trip, especially if you are having an uneventful Christmas on your own, or at your parents' house.

If you are spending Christmas Day under far less exciting circumstances than you believe he is—or in a less salubrious place than he is at—then it will be pure hell for you. You are only human, after all! Be prepared to feel jealous, cheated, and taken for a fool as you sweat it out until he gets back—or until he calls to tell you how much he's missing you. *Yawn!*

The anger will manifest itself (and I *do* have to speak to you once more as though you are in love with your MM—otherwise you won't give a hoot where he is and what he's doing) because throughout the year, you will have listened to all the lines and the lies he has fed you about his situation. (In fact, I'm sure many of you will have listened to the entire content of this book fall from his duplicitous lips in some shape or form.) You will have heard about how he'd *like* to change things to be with you, *if only* he could. And how he and his wife have *no* chemistry, *no* passion. *(Oh, puh-leeze!)*

✎ **NOTE TO PATIENT MARTYRS OF MISTRESSES:** If he has taken his family skiing for Christmas (just for the sake of the children, of course, not because he wants to go for one minute), you could well sit alone, wondering not only if he's "out on the piste" with his wife but if he's beginning to "take the piste" with you!

Depending on your circumstances as a mistress, and how good or bad you feel your affair is, Christmas can be quite a landmark in the other woman's calendar. For some, it can be a big, stark smack in the teeth—a harsh note to self that he has done nothing but procrastinate for the previous twelve months. He may have told you that he wants to leave his wife to be with you, plans to do it at some point (blah, blah), and has been successful in keeping you hanging on that string, but the reality is that here you are at the closing of the year, wanting to be with him (and believing him when he echoes your sentiment). Yet—hello? It wasn't *you* he woke up with on the twenty-fifth of December, was it, sister? He is still with someone else!

✎ **NOTE:** This is a form of passive-aggressive behavior, which is typical in a married man. He *appears* to be good to you—kind and loving on the surface—yet ultimately he does all the things you hate and that make you unhappy. (A bit like having a mother who says she loves you so much but each day cuts off one of your fingers. You'd be confused to say the least!)

If this is you, and the holiday season brings this daunting realization to you, then you will most likely feel cheated. You will also feel angry that you've attached yourself to someone who can make you feel like this. You might be annoyed at yourself about the reasons why you just can't walk away. This could come down to the fact that you think he is *so* close to leaving his wife and that you are too near the goal to leave him quite yet.

✎ NOTE TO MISTRESSES IN THIS TYPE OF QUANDARY: In a nutshell, while you are enduring all these emotions, your Christmas can easily be overlooked if you continue to obsess about what he is doing (and, more to the point, why he isn't doing it *with you*). You will have to go through the motions of enjoying yourself if you're with family and friends, but inside you will want it all to be over as soon as possible, so you can get back to work and normality—and hence, distraction.

☞ HARSH NOTE TO MISTRESSES: Stop right here, right now! For God's sake, don't give him the satisfaction of making you feel miserable by keeping you in limbo all the time. If you're going to be the mistress, try to put a fun, festive spin on all this, so that the positives of being the other woman outweigh the negatives (at least for the sake of your seasonal sanity anyway). Let me give you some plus points to mull over…

The biggest and most obvious positive to "mistressdom" is that you should be well taken care of all year round and spoiled with lots of lovely things to enhance your lifestyle. At Christmas this should be paramount. You should receive lots of wonderful presents from your MM, commonly known as "guilt gifts" (and don't even consider holding back on your list to Santa, as his wife won't be, that's for sure).

Furthermore, let's acknowledge that there are many similarities between being a mistress and being a full-fledged SUW. Whether throughout the year or just at special occasions like Christmas, when you think about it, there really isn't much tangible difference between both your singleton lifestyles, is there?

Surviving Christmas as a Mistress
And Other Holidays

NOTE TO MISTRESSES: Apart from a few expensive Christmas gifts from an MM, of course… *Ho ho ho!*

TIP FOR SUWs: Try to bag yourself a man for the season if you can—just to buy you a few "pressies" to go under your little tree. He doesn't have to be for life, *just for Christmas.* Failing that, spend the money, which you don't need to waste on gifts for a nonexistent significant other, on *yourself.* Enjoy your hard-earned cash to your heart's content…after all, you're worth it! You are totally fabulous and deserve the best—always remember that!

So both a mistress and an SUW live *alone*, shop *alone*, drink *alone*, and sleep *alone*, and their single status goes toward the demographic statistic of single people living within our society today.

NOTE TO SELF: Actually, there is one *big* difference between the single woman and the other woman. Whilst the single Bridget Jones–type women of today may experience bouts of utter despair and depression at not being able to meet a "life partner"—called Mr. Darcy or whatever else—the mistress in love is *guaranteed* this daily despair and doom by already having met a part-time partner who won't leave *his* "life partner." The mistress can also add *extra* bouts of heartache and angst in varying quantities to her daily dose.

TIME-MANAGEMENT NOTE: Whilst fighting this depression, being an SUW or a mistress means you won't have to make any extra time to do somebody's washing, ironing, or cleaning. You can focus purely on being miserable.

Another huge similarity between the SUW and the mistress is their limited list of groceries to shop for and the parallel contents of their fridges, as both the SUW and the mistress will generally be shopping and eating for one.

ANOTHER POSITIVE NOTE: This makes occasions like Christmas dead easy, and far cheaper than if you were shopping to prepare some kind of wonderful, traditional festive lunch with all the trimmings for loads of hungry people!

Both the SUW's and the mistress's shopping lists will undoubtedly contain a selection of "meals for one"—the staple food of single people.

✎ **NOTE TO SELF:** I don't know why manufacturers assume that if you happen to be single, and thus eating alone, you have absolutely no sense of taste. They must, though, considering the type of rubbery, tasteless frozen food items they produce in fancy cardboard boxes *(you know the ones)*.

Those tempting pictures of dishes that reel us in under the auspices of the tasty cuisine we're familiar with—things like chicken parmesan or shepherd's pie—are a real swiz. In reality, when you've followed the instructions and microwaved the small, overly priced offering for five to six minutes on the highest setting (remembering, of course, to pull back the clear plastic film and stir halfway through), it bears no resemblance in taste nor appearance to its namesake, even when you *have* let it stand for those three minutes before serving!

✎ **"DING" NOTE REFERENCE:** I generally refer to this type of "cuisine" as "ding food" in homage to single people everywhere, and in honor of the noise the microwave makes to let you know when the food is ready to eat *(and hot enough to burn your mouth on).*

✎ **A PRACTICAL NOTE ABOUT BEING SINGLE:** You can have a hot, square meal ready in less than eight minutes (although you may need asbestos lips to eat it), and with absolutely NO dishes to have to take care of afterward. *Ding-dong, sisters!* (At Christmas feel free to kick it up a notch as you "Ding Dong Merrily On High.")

An SUW may well shop for certain *special* grocery items to impress any potential ad hoc dates she projects having and bringing home without warning (especially at the weekend). Similarly, a good mistress may also shop for those special items her MM likes if she thinks he's coming over (which will *never* be at the weekend).

✎ **OBSERVATIONAL NOTE:** When neither woman is shopping for items to impress possible male visitors, the contents of both their fridges will, on a day-to-day basis, generally resemble a third-world country—i.e., sparse!

With regards to drinking alone, that can become a little boring (or normal, depending how you look at it), but if you live alone, there is little other option, is there?

Y SUBSTANCE ABUSE NOTE: You hear it said that a person has a potential addiction problem if he or she starts drinking alone. But if, as I have proven here, single women and mistresses live a pretty solitary life and do most everything alone, why on earth should there be any stigma attached to the recreational drinking part of it? It is *purely* circumstantial, so I refuse to buy into that one.

Drinking can be regarded as company to some. And for many mistresses, depending on their particular situation and their grasp on the affair, drinking can act as a painkiller and a sleeping tablet all in one. (Those in need of both, due to the velocity of their affair, will know exactly what I mean by this.) Alcohol can be viewed as a portable vacation for many mistresses—a chance to switch off!

✎ NOTE TO POTENTIAL ALCOHOLICS AND PAINKILLER ADDICTS: Watch out for this! Try not to become reliant on the old "sauce," as it could be your downfall should you plan to meet a single guy for a regular relationship. An addiction to the suppressant alcohol provides will be hard to shake loose, even if you do happen to move on and meet a wonderful man who doesn't want to hurt you.

✎ A POSITIVE NOTE ABOUT LIVING AND DRINKING ALONE: You don't need to share your liquor with *anyone* (heaven knows, it's not cheap these days), plus nobody can see how wasted you get of an evening and scream at you when you fall over on your way to bed (nor chastise you if you decide to sleep on the sofa all night).

So we've discussed eating and drinking alone, but how about sleeping alone? It *can* become really tedious, but this is debatable depending upon what type of affair you're having and what your expectations are.

✎ NOTE TO SUWs: As you're single, you have no expectations and you are used to sleeping alone, so I will be addressing mistresses here.

If the mistress is *not* in love, she will generally be indifferent as to when and how she sleeps with her MM. She may casually look forward to whatever liaison they have planned, but she won't be stressing over it either way. However, for the mistress in love with her MM, the sleeping alone part (whilst he is sleeping with another woman) will be an absolute killer!

✎ **GENERAL POSITIVITY SPIN NOTE TO ALL WOMEN SLEEPING ALONE:** You don't need to make *any* effort when you go to bed to look or smell great. You can wear your oldest T-shirt and your thickest face cream—*who is there to care?*

✎ **REALITY NOTE:** Sometimes it would be nice if there *was* someone there to care. *Sigh. . .*

Okay, so back to Christmas—a time when you should be with people you love and who love you. The sentiment is all around you, pretty much from the end of summer until the end of December, constantly fueled by frequent colorful store advertisements of happy, beautiful people jumping around in cheery, warm, cozy clothing and matching mittens. The plethora of feel-good holiday songs and movies back up this seasonal propaganda, depicting just how much *fun* it is to be in love at Christmas and ramming it down our throats. All further compounded by those annoying "perfect gift ideas" for that "special person" in your life—these will be paraded in your face nonstop, especially on the television.

✎ **NOTE TO ADVERTISERS:** How about making a reality advert that reflects how life actually is, eh? How about a cheating married man trying to decide what gift to buy his wife and what gift to buy his mistress—and more to the point, which one he spends the most money on (or, God forbid, even gets them both the same thing).

At the end of the day, for mistresses who are in love, there is no way to get around Christmas, nor escape it and all that comes with it. So to revert back to my original positive slant on all of this—make sure you get some nice gifts from him. It will help dull the pain. A nice little sports car will keep you busy, for example.

✎ **NOTE TO CHRISTMAS MISTRESSES:** If you're lucky, Christmas Eve will become "your" Christmas Day with your MM, your private time together. And if you've been a good girl all year, he will undoubtedly have a "full sack" waiting for you!

Mistresses, you will be full of mixed emotions as Christmas draws near. You will hopefully be full of the Christmas cheer, office parties, and pre-Christmas things one looks forward to and enjoys on the lead-up to the big day. Part of the fun will be enjoying some pre-festive times with your MM. Due to the nature of the situation, you and your married lover already know you won't be seeing each other during Christmas, so you will naturally try to do some of the nice things together in advance, those things you can't actually do on the day. You may both try to overcompensate with things like Christmas tree dressing, shopping, dinners, movies, and so on. You, as the mistress, will love all of this and want more. Consequently, it will make you want to spend *all* of Christmas with him!

✎ **NOTE OF WARNING TO PRE-CHRISTMAS MISTRESSES IN LOVE:** Try not to enjoy these activities together too much, because if you let yourself get all sentimental and *used to* the feeling of having a man around at Christmas, you will be in for a huge shock when suddenly—*wham!*—you don't see or hear from him from December 25 (or at least *hardly* hear from him) until New Year's is over. Even though you thought you were mentally prepared and okay with it all, it is an entirely different ball game when it actually happens. His telephonic silence can be quite deafening.

Following on from that will be the second part of your "yuletide double whammy," as not only will you not hear from him, but you will start to obsess over your MM and *his* Christmas (with his wife). You will literally convince yourself that he is spending a wonderful, perfect, happy time with his family, even if in truth it's not *that* wonderful for him. You will totally persuade yourself that he is "having a ball" and his bells are being jingled.

🔔 **NOTE TO MISTRESSES:** Anyone jingling your bells?

If you don't have children of your own, you will also obsess about him and his wife sharing the closeness that kids bring them at Christmas. You will wonder if your MM and his wife woke up in the same bed on Christmas morning (whatever he tells you his sleeping arrangements are, and *just* for the sake of the kids, of course). You'll fantasize about whether they stayed up late to drink mulled wine and wrap presents for their little ones (well, that's what all those holiday adverts would have us believe, no?). You may also beat yourself up over whether they had sex after becoming *so much closer* at this time of year. (Hey, by the way, all those feel-good holiday movies you went to see alone don't help your cause and frame of mind you know!)

🖉 **A VERY POSITIVE CALORIFIC NOTE:** Whilst you are obsessing over all of this, you will be too depressed *(and far too drunk)* to eat any of the chocolate you got for Christmas and therefore won't run the risk of piling on any extra pounds. Meanwhile, his indifferent wife, who hasn't got a care in the world *(in your eyes!)* will be relaxed enough to chow down on all the wonderful chocolate boxes she received from her husband. Let her chunk up on your behalf, as a wife can never be too fat *(in your eyes)*.

Whether a true SUW or indeed a mistress, Christmas always tends to bring with it a sharp wake-up call to both categories of women. It is a slap in the face from "old Nick" that marks the closure of yet another biologically ticking year in the egg timer of one's childbearing shelf life.

🖉 **NOTE TO SINGLE WOMEN:** It annoyingly alerts you to the fact that the same time last year, you had assured yourself that you would definitely be spending the next Christmas with the man of your dreams, convincing yourself you had a good twelve months ahead of you to find him!

🖉 **NOTE TO MISTRESSES IN LOVE:** It depressingly alerts you to the fact that this time last year, you had assured yourself he would definitely be all yours by next Christmas, convincing yourself you had a good twelve months ahead of you to get him!

Mistresses, you may have also vowed that if he didn't leave *her* by the next Christmas, you would be off! Big words, but, hey ho, here you are, still hanging in there! You're the one still waiting on the sidelines while he lives his life on the stage.

🖉 **NOTE TO MISTRESSES:** Please don't wait on the sidelines. Keep your options open just like he does. Use the run up to Christmas to meet other men, but try to stay away from the married ones (although at Christmas it's hard because they're everywhere—*it's like an epidemic*).

Most single women have festive fantasies of how they'd like their Christmas to be *(so do a lot of married ones, actually!)*, relaxing and canoodling in front of a fire with their wonderful man, who is wearing a chunky, hand-knitted red Christmas scarf, which looks so dashing next to his healthy pink cheeks (I mean the ones on his face— *naughty!*). The snow falls outside the window as you clink those decadently oversized wine glasses together, full of that expensive red wine, in a toast to the holidays and to your future.

✎ **FESTIVE REALITY NOTE:** Unfortunately, the only clinking likely to take place for a "Christmas Mistress" is the *fizz* and *plop* acoustics when she drops a paracetamol tablet into a glass of water to cure the hangover from too much soul-searching the previous night.

⚷ **TIP FOR MISTRESSES (AND SUWs):** If you want to clink with yourself, make sure you do it against something that can offer you a good clink back—like a brick wall or another empty glass.

If you are a mistress on Christmas Day, you may find it hard to cope with the neverending, punishing thoughts of what you imagine him to be doing with his family as opposed to what you wish *you* were doing with him.

And as you lay there on the sofa in your sweatpants, exhausted from microwaving a turkey dinner for one, while watching the reruns of last year's Christmas shows and checking your cell phone constantly, hoping for a call or a text message from him—*anything* to send you a signal that he's thinking about you and needing to reach out to you, and therefore *not* having the wonderful time you imagined—you may wonder, "How can he just switch off like this?" Right? You may begin to ponder if it is worth being this poor, sad, lonely mistress pining for her MM or whether it would be better to just be a fully fledged singleton—period! (Therefore eliminating the heartache, pondering, wondering, and pining of having an MM in the equation.)

✎ **NOTE TO MELANCHOLY MISTRESSES ON THE SOFA:**
The answer to this will depend largely on the quality and quantity of gifts he bought you. *(Well, let's stay real about it!)*

For all those women flying solo at Christmas, the following table may help you weigh up the question of being an SUW versus a mistress, as it shows some comparisons of what you think you want at Christmas (i.e., to be part of a couple) versus the advantages of what you do have (i.e., *not* being part of a couple).

FANTASIES OF BEING A COUPLE	BENEFITS OF BEING A MISTRESS
Waking up early Christmas morning next to your lover.	Getting up at whatever time you feel like (if at all).
Wearing that fabulous sexy new lingerie and nightwear you bought for the special day, to impress your man.	Feeling completely relaxed in your ancient ugly pajamas (which you never let your MM see).
Making love before you both open all your thoughtfully purchased and well-wrapped gifts, along with the surprise stockings full of goodies, which are hanging up at the end of the bed.	Not having to have to have sex if you don't feel like it and not having to pretend you like the wrong gifts he got you. (Savvy mistresses can just play with the money their MM gave them for Christmas instead.)
Enjoying a sumptuous breakfast thoughtfully prepared by your lover and brought to you in bed, as you recline against plump, white linen feather pillows and enjoy the freshly ground coffee and freshly squeezed orange juice made by his own fair hand.	Reaching for the vodka bottle, which you thoughtfully didn't finish off the night before, and demolishing the last slice of pizza left in the refrigerator. A perfect no fuss, no mess breakfast for one, which you can easily enjoy in bed (as nobody is there to witness the grunge of it all!).

FANTASIES OF BEING A COUPLE	BENEFITS OF BEING A MISTRESS
Smelling the turkey roasting in the family kitchen as you listen to Dean Martin's Christmas album.	Trying out a new flavor of meal- for-one selections in your freezer, while you watch reruns of *Will and Grace*.
Wearing that new Christmas outfit and preparing for the arrival of your happily married friends, and non-dysfunctional family members, for lunch. Drinking a glass of wine as you cook together with your man, working as a loving team.	Staying in your pajamas while lounging around watching movies and drinking the whole bottle of wine yourself. Alternatively, you should try to bag yourself a Christmas luncheon invite.
Topping up your mother-in-law's wine glass to ensure she falls asleep in front of the TV after all that turkey. Thus leaving you quality time together with your man while showing him just how caring and loving you are toward his mother at the same time. (Two birds with one stone, so to speak.)	Not needing to give a hoot about anybody's damned mother, nor waste your wine on her either. **NOTE TO PAJAMA-CLAD MISTRESSES:** Better to focus on topping up your own glass so that you can fall asleep in front of the TV. (That way the day will be over much quicker.)
Pulling Christmas crackers and laughing with your guests over coffee and dessert, as your man helps you clear the table and the kitchen, profusely thanking you in front of everyone for the wonderful lunch you prepared and saying how proud he is of you. *(Er, hello? What the hell kind of world do you live in?)*	Throwing away the plastic container and empty box that your meal for one came in—or in the case of those smart ones who bagged an invite, helping to clear a few plates from your host's table before leaving them to go home to the peace of your singleton apartment, where you can go *snap, crackle,* and *pop* on your sofa, as you *are* a real little Christmas cracker.
Being paranoid and worried about being kept in the dark while your other half goes to secretly call his mistress behind your back.	Not needing to worry about being kept in the dark, as YOU are the mistress, and you'll take his call with glad tidings of joy!

Now, on to another sensitive, soul-searching time of the holiday season—New Year's Eve. For those mistresses who have already lived through a particularly difficult Christmas, a typical New Year's resolution might be to terminate that dead-end affair, promising to focus *much harder* on finding an available counterpart, one who will be there for you, love you, and definitely not leave you for another woman at Christmas.

✎ **NOTE TO SAVVY MISTRESSES AT NEW YEAR'S:** At the stroke of midnight, you should question whether your duplicitous MM is raising his glass to his wife, hugging her and making some shared New Year's resolutions together for the coming year. Or whether he's in that *terribly* difficult situation of being with the family, and indeed sleeping in the spare room.

🗝 **TIP:** Try asking him next time you see him!

Now, ladies, if you *are* serious about trying to find your future Mr. Right, you might be considering changing some of your criteria and compromising in a few areas—thoughts of trading down, trading up, not setting your goals so high, not coming across as too needy, and definitely not looking desperate *(heaven forbid!)* may be entering your head (although it sounds like you might be undergoing a personality transplant just to find him!).

✎ **NOTE TO MISTRESSES:** Your attitude about life and men will depend largely on whether you've been left feeling unhappy and despondent by the way your MM treated you during Christmas. But as you can see, with so many agendas to consider when actually looking for another man to replace him, it's easy to see why we keep gravitating back to dating the married ones, as they are *so* desperate, they will take you as you are…even if you are desperate too!

✎ **POSITIVE NOTE ABOUT DATING AN MM AS OPPOSED TO A SINGLE ONE:** A single, available man with good prospects won't usually take on a desperate, complex woman (unless he's really ugly or broke, and who needs *that*), whereas the MMs will always take anything they can get (and they know the crazy chicks will be great at sex). Generally, MMs are more grateful in bed than single ones, and the older they are, the far more grateful they are!

In order to further your *mission impossible* of meeting someone available, and to rid yourself of the MM curse, you may consider speed dating, online dating, blind dating, in fact, any-God-damned dating, as a way of bringing you closer to your goal of a *partner*, thus ending a life in the land of ding food forever—finally becoming whole and complete as one half of a loving, successful relationship. (Yeah, yeah, I know—it only seems to happen to other people.)

✎ **NOTE TO MISTRESSES:** This is exactly why a mistress tends to stay in her affair—because although she has a wish list and criteria for her ideal partner, as we proved early in this book, there is a severe shortage of unmarried men that unmarried women would want to make a life with. Such a severe shortage, in fact, that it's almost becoming a national disaster. Nothing better, and single, ever seems to come along (or we are too busy being complex and confused to even see it if it does?).

So lastly, to get off the depressing subject of spending Christmas as a mistress, let's take a quick look at Valentine's Day and an article I read last year about a survey carried out in a top New York restaurant. It boasted double the business on the evening of February 13 than on the following night, on the occasion of Valentine's Day.

Based on the type of clientele that was dining, the restaurant owners put it down to the fact that a higher percentage of men dined out with their mistresses (apparently it was very obvious) on the thirteenth, as opposed to the following night, when the cheating MMs knew they would be *stuck* with their wives.

The staff also noted that the atmosphere on the thirteenth was far more lighthearted and fun than it was on the fourteenth, when few words and many scowls were the only things being easily exchanged at most of the tables.

✎ **NOTE TO MISTRESSES:** Make sure your MM takes you somewhere really fancy on either Valentine's Day or the night before. (If it falls on a weekend, you will need to compromise, but do it directly before or afterward so he is unable to get out of it.) Make sure you do it, and do it in style, because Valentine's Day should be the most important day of the year in a mistress's diary! Don't let that responsibility slip his mind along with the rest.

GENERAL RECAP NOTES OF ADVICE FOR MISTRESSES:

- I hope this chapter has helped in some small way. There is no way to be totally generic on this subject, and remember these are only *my* opinions and observations (it doesn't mean they're right). Each mistress will feel differently than the next about her situation, and will be in a different type of an affair with a different type of MM than the next. But I think I can speak for any woman who has been, or is, a mistress in love with a married man—it is extremely painful on certain occasions. You know how lonely and low some of the most "happy occasions" can leave you feeling.

- Try to make the best of it or get out, as you really *do* have a choice, although you will convince yourself that you can't end the affair because you love him. Even though you will be experiencing the low self-esteem we talked about, nobody is forcing you to stay with a man who is married and isn't with you during these times when you obviously want him to be.

- Try to use these times—Christmas and the New Year especially—as a benchmark to take stock of things. Take a look at what *you* want out of life and out of him. You may be surprised at what you come up with. You owe it to yourself at least to try!

- Articulate to your MM how hard these times are for you. See if he can make more time in which you can be together during special occasions. (You know the answer will be NO, but it's good to stress him out over it. Don't *always* be "accepting" of everything.)

- If all else fails, try to make these happy occasions as miserable as possible for him—things like calling him off the hook, and sending him unpleasant text messages and e-mails, threatening to end the affair if he doesn't leave her. (I'd try to stay clear of calling his house to wish him and his wife a very merry Christmas and all the best for the New Year, though...)
- Remember in all of this to be strong. Your day will come, with or without him, as I am sure you're a wonderful, desirable woman who is selling herself short by settling for the trauma and stress that this chapter has exposed.

chapter 12

"I'll Call You Later"

Bet You He Won't!

So, mistresses, I wanted to end this book with something you'll hear all the time. (No, silly—*not* the "I'm not sleeping with my wife!" line.) This is something else you'll hear your MM say all the time: "I'll call you later."

You will probably welcome this signing-off statement, as in my experience a mistress loves talking to her MM as much as possible and vice versa. In fact, they can never get enough of each other, and the phone calls are a huge part of their lives.

Your MM will say this a lot, on a number of levels and on different types of occasions. However, he will never know just how deeply it resonates with you when he says it, but doesn't do it.

If he is about to enter into his "other life" (with his wife), this "call you later" statement gives him the get-out clause he needs to placate you, as he knows he won't be able to call you later when he's home with her. Also, it's a nice way *for him* of never having closure with you when he talks to you on the phone. Because think about it, mistresses. "I'll call you later," said to you either on the phone or in person, as your MM is about to drive home, or board a plane, or whatever he needs to do in order to get back to his wife and family, will sound much better than "Bye-bye, I'll call you tomorrow because I can't call you tonight from the house. We're having a dinner party for twelve people, and I haven't seen my wife all week so I do need to give her some quality time." *(See where I'm coming from?)* Even if he says, "I'll *try* to call you later," it's still better than having to hear about his forthcoming family activities, don't you think?

✎ **NOTE OF FAIRNESS ON AN MM's BEHALF** *(rare from me):* Many times an MM will mean it when he says "I'll call you later." Sometimes it's not calculated, and it could genuinely be that he just doesn't get around to calling you back. (He might well have been tied up with his family, or he might really have just forgotten to call you.) It may have totally slipped his mind that he even told you he would (remember, he won't hang on his every word like you do). And also remember, he's got a lot of people and things making demands on him and his time—work, kids, wife, golf, tennis, and so on. It's not *all* about his mistress, you know! (Well, not when it isn't convenient for him, anyway!)

Being a mistress is all about waiting for calls from your MM. (Yes, and texts and e-mails too, but mainly calls.) Calls to say he loves you, calls to tell you he misses you and needs to see you as soon as possible, late-night calls to tell you he wants phone sex, calls to ask you to have dinner with him a week from Tuesday or to invite you on a business trip to New York with him. Whatever the topic, a mistress will wait for an MM's calls far, far more than she ever would from a regular, unmarried boyfriend.

☎ **NOTE TO MISTRESSES WAITING FOR CALLS:** I would say that this is due to the fact that most of the time you know that a call from your MM usually brings with it the initiation of a plan to see each other.

But the downside for many mistresses *in love*—oh, what the hell. I can mention love freely now. I'm on the last chapter, and we all know we fall in love with certain married men far more than available ones, so let's not be in denial for the last few pages!—is that when he doesn't call, you may have a tendency to obsess over the reasons as to why.

"I'll Call You Later"
Bet You He Won't!

If you know he is *en famille*, you will wonder why he couldn't find five minutes to go out to the backyard and call you, like he has before. This may lead you to question if he's cooling down on you or perhaps if things are "hotting up" for him at home (although any married person will tell you that once a marriage starts to slide, it never "hots up" again—it usually just gets worse!).

🖎 **NOTE TO MISTRESSES:** The first six months of the affair is when he will be at his hottest for you, and the sexual relationship he is enjoying with you will be at its peak. After that, whilst he certainly won't want the sexual part of it to end, he will *not* be thinking along the lines of upsetting his happy home for you (even though he may well still be telling you he's planning to. *Yawn!*).

If he is unreachable because his phone is constantly switched off and keeps going to voice mail, this will compound the obsessive fanatical scenarios you are letting play out in your head about why he's too busy to call you.

If you happen to have left him a voice mail on, say, Friday evening and he hasn't returned it by Sunday lunchtime… *Whoosh!* That's like a red flag to a bull, because the over-inquiring mind of a mistress could well assume he is having too much family fun to be bothered to call his "bit on the side." The one he just likes to have sex with during the week!

🖎 **NOTE TO MISTRESSES:** Those feelings of low self-esteem and cheapness we've discussed may come back to haunt you in this situation. You could feel annoyed that you're good enough for sex but *not* good enough to make a proper life with (like he has with his wife—or so you convince yourself, anyway). Also remember my words about a mistress helping to make the MM happier at home, and in general, hence his wife reaping the benefits too!

But how about this scenario *(this is a good one…you'll like it)*— what if he has been honest with you, which we like, and told you he's going to be home for the entire boring weekend and will call you when he can, but that it might be difficult. And what if you buy into that?

You're cool, and you get on with your life, going about your business, and looking forward to speaking to him when he comes out of his guilt weekend. Therefore not relying on his call at all.

You are in a good place, offsetting the pleasure of knowing that he will be bored with *her* (and that's one thing you know he *never* is when he's with you). But then...what if he does call you, needing to do it sneakily, because he's out with his wife somewhere enjoying—or enduring—a weekend social activity. He may have had a few drinks too many and is missing you.

You might initially be glad he called, but boy will you be pissed off that he's enjoying a social outing with his wife, while you are sitting at home waiting—just in case he *did* call you later after all! (You know he always tries your home number before your mobile, and because if he can't talk, you like to make things quicker and easier for him, right?) This will be especially maddening because he told you that they never go out much as a couple. *(Ha! Hello?)* So in the big picture, you might end up feeling so down about the fact that he *did* call, and *is* out and about with his Mrs., that in truth it would have been better if he'd never "called you later" at all!

Another occasion when he might sneakily "call you later" is, say, from a birthday dinner he's throwing for his wife at a noisy restaurant, or while he's with her on holiday somewhere, or spending the weekend with their friends for an anniversary get-together, or similar. You name it! You need to be prepared for this, because they are living as a married couple, and this is what married couples do.

Your MM may well call you from all sorts of locations and events (whilst with his wife) as often as he can, simply because wherever he is is probably boring for him. And whatever he's doing he'd probably rather be having fun with you, *especially* in that first six months. But the question is, would you rather he call and know that he is thinking of you—and revel in the fact that his wife is boring him? Or would you rather he not call because you'll fantasize and create scenarios when you realize how annoyed you are that he *is* doing stuff with his wife? (Things you may not have been obsessing about at all, before he called you and reminded you!)

As usual, his call to you will help *him*, but it may not help you. (I urge you not to always help him.) He may well tell you that you have no need to feel jealous about where he is because "there is certainly nothing to be jealous of," and how he would much *rather* be with you. But the bottom line is that he isn't, is he? He's with *her*—proof, pudding, and all that!

✒ **TIP FOR MISTRESSES:** Let him be bored. Be a bit unobtainable. Tell him you were doing something *really* exciting (with someone else maybe?). Lie to him. After all, it's the fashion!

As you can see—and surely agree—it's not just about the statement "I'll call you later." It's actually about the whole bag of connotations it opens up, allowing you extra opportunity and reasons to stress if he doesn't call.

You might be a mistress who will hang on his "calling you later" more than he can *or should ever* know. You will use it as a benchmark against his activities and against his allotted family time at home.

If he doesn't call you when he made a point of saying he would, *especially* if he committed to a reason for his "call later"—such as "I'll call you in an hour when I'm alone," or "I'll call you to say goodnight," or "I'll call to wake you up in the morning"—then he's building up trouble with you. I'm sure as a savvy mistress you will keep your cool in the beginning because you wouldn't want to look clingy or neurotic *(not so soon into your affair, anyway)*. But the closer the two of you become, the more this statement that rolls *so easily* off his tongue might become his worst enemy.

If you take it upon yourself to call him when he *doesn't* "call you later" (so as not to let him off the hook), and if his mobile happens to be switched off, it will end up frustrating you beyond words. You will overthink what he might be doing with his wife, or even another mistress. (Otherwise, why would he need to switch his phone off?) It will drive you goddamn crazy, especially because you know, more than anyone, that his phone is usually switched off when he's up to no good (i.e., *when he's with you*), so you will fantasize, glamorize, and create scenarios that are more than likely blown out of all proportion (or not?). Even worse is if he answers but puts the phone down, or pretends he can't hear you when he knows it's you on the other end.

✎ **NOTE TO MISTRESSES:** You will no doubt place sex high on your list within your affair; it's an important factor between you and your MM. But you shouldn't get into the mindset that it's important to everyone. Don't use your relationship with him as a yardstick for what you *think* he does with his wife. A lot of women really aren't into sex—she's probably one of them, at least not with her husband, *your MM,* anyway!

When he does finally switch his phone back on and allows you back into his life and calls you, you will either be pleased to hear from him or so frustrated by his "other life" that you let rip with your anger. How you converse with him during those periods when he's with his wife will give him a clue as to whether you are a "bunny boiler," or not (his barometer as to whether you are likely to go nuts on him, and his wife, in the future).

✎ **NOTE TO MISTRESSES:** Always keep that thought in your head, because it is a very real (usually unspoken) point of reference for any married man who has seen the movie *Fatal Attraction.*

If your MM has been with the wife all weekend and has had limited, if any, contact with you, trying to reconnect on Monday could be hard for you.

✎ **NOTE TO MISTRESSES:** Your MM certainly won't find it hard to reconnect with you; he will be looking forward immensely to calling you after his weekend of domesticity. And he will be totally and utterly oblivious to any pain and anguish he may have caused you through his day-to-day actions of running his life. It'll be *your* call as to whether you bite the bullet and let rip, or toe the line for a quiet life and more gifts.

"I'll Call You Later"
Bet You He Won't!

If he had any sense, he would realize that it is naturally very hard for you to pick up where you left off with someone who has spent the weekend with another woman (of course, this applies only if you love him). You wouldn't accept it in a normal relationship, would you? Yet you are doing so here. You are accepting it because he tells you he *has to* do it. He has brainwashed and indoctrinated you into going along with it all in order to be with him.

✎ **NOTE TO MISTRESSES:** Do you *really* want to be in a relationship where you have to keep disconnecting with "your" man?

He will want his mistress to react less, but it is a no-win situation (and more of the passive-aggressive emotional abuse), because whilst he keeps going back to his wife and cutting you off, you keep hurting and building up resentment toward him by the time he calls. You are rotting inside while you wait for him, and you go mad all weekend and can't concentrate on anything else until you "give him a piece of your mind." So by the time he calls you on Monday, you are about to burst, and you cannot possibly interact with him as the person he wants you to be—i.e., breezy, upbeat, and not at all angry.

✎ **NOTE TO MISTRESSES:** You will probably feel very alone in your relationship, so you might as well be. What's the difference? Only heartache to keep you company. *Who needs that!*

He will keep fueling you with stories that he doesn't love his wife, and is not sleeping with her—which he will naturally *think* you want to hear, and maybe you do. But conversely, what's the point, as nothing ever gets done about it, does it? He's ultimately shooting himself in the foot with his information, and in the end, when you give him an ultimatum (MMs hate ultimatums from their mistresses, and the wives never issue them—*they don't care enough*), you probably won't see him for dust!

To those MMs who haven't been *overly* vocal about things during your affair—who haven't told such in-depth lies as some of the others we've talked about—their get-out clause will probably be, "Well, you *knew* I was married. I never promised you anything!"

RECAP NOTES FOR MISTRESSES:

- Your MM *may* mean it when he says "I'll call you later." If he does and he can, he will in fact do so.
- He may say it and have absolutely no intention of meaning it, as he knows he will be ensconced in something at home by the time he plans to call you.
- Sadly, a mistress will hang on to the fact that her MM was *going to call.*

✎ **FINAL NOTE TO MISTRESSES:** Even if the affair ends badly (note to MMs: you should be *very wary* of that happening), the law of averages is that he will *always* come back to you at some point, especially if the affair was particularly intense, as he won't be able to just erase the memories, along with your phone number.

Even if the breakup was awful and you said things you thought not humanly possible to recover from (and, yes, even if you *did* call his wife and expose him as a two-timing liar and cheating bastard—and he decided to stay with her and *she let him stay),* he will still "call you later" because he will never really *ever* get over you. He will never be able to get you out of his head, period!

So after the dust has settled and his boring little marriage is back on its boring little path again, you will *constantly* be back on his mind (not that you ever left it to begin with, of course).

So there we have it, sisters. The call from your ex-MM can come anywhere from six months to two years down the line. But after an affair is over, you can literally set your mental stopwatch because you know he will always "call you later." More importantly, though—will you *still* be waiting around for him as if you had nothing better to do with your life?

THE END
(Or maybe…*just the beginning?)*

Glossary of Terms

Aarrgh: Aarrgh!

Angina heartstrings: A dodgy ticker

Boxes have been ticked: When his or her criteria have been checked

Bunny boiler: A mistress when she goes nuts (reference to the movie *Fatal Attraction*)

CML: Cheapskate married lover

DD: Due diligence

Ding food: Microwaved food that single people live on

Dodgy ticker: A weak heart; angina or panic attacks

Financial paraplegic: An MM going through a divorce

Ghostwifer: A mistress who plays a big part in the outcome of her MM's marriage

Home *en famille:* When the MM is at home with his family

Hotting up: Getting more exciting

Ka-ching: The sound of a wife's "cash register" (i.e., her vagina)

Lame old chestnut of an excuse: A poor, unbelievable lie

(To) Lie for England: Lying well enough for a whole country

Love cocktail stage: The dreamy, heady time before the lies set in

MM: Married man
MMMMM: A multi-multi-millionaire married man
Mental gymnastics: Overthinking and obsessive thoughts in an affair
Mental wrist slashing: Trauma caused by cruel thoughts of an MM
           with his wife
Mistress: Woman enjoying sex with somebody else's husband
Mousewife: A doormat of a wife
Onus: To put the responsibility on someone else
Peachy: Happy and nice
Red flag to a bull: A danger signal; something that alerts one
SHF: Short-haul fornication
SUW: Single unmarried woman
Spare room scenario: When the MM professes not to be sleeping
           with his wife
Swan in and swan out: An MM that breezes in and out as he pleases
Willy-nilly: Something said without any thought or weight behind it

Bonus Sayings:

Descriptions used when one half of a relationship/marriage refers to the other half as not turning him or her on sexually

"He or she just…"
- doesn't turn my screw
- doesn't float my boat
- doesn't light my candle
- doesn't wind my clock
- doesn't blow my whistle
- doesn't swing my hammock

www.havinganaffairthebook.com